See What Moms and Othe
Are Saying About *Coach Mom*

"If you're needing help keeping your sanity in the world of motherhood and wifedom, this is the book for you!"
—*Thelma Wells, speaker and author for Women of Faith*

"*Coach Mom* supports, simplifies, and celebrates the journey of mothers."
—*Jennifer Rothschild, Jennifer Rothschild Ministries*

"Mothers and families across America should read this book and put into practice Brenna's great and practical advice. We'll have super families as folks, young and old, become a Coach Mom."
—*Dal Shealy, executive director, Fellowship of Christian Athletes, Football Coaches Ministry*

"This is just the help every young mother needs. *Coach Mom* will help you enjoy raising the next godly generation!"
—*Esther Burroughs, mother, grandmother, and author*

"The book that I thought would teach me about the inside of my home really became the journey of the inside of my heart and faith…. My home and heart will never be the same."
—*Lesley Bain*

"You have made a tremendous difference in the quality of my day-to-day life…. You have lightened my load!"
—*Deeann Rippee*

"You've made me laugh 'til I cried—when I most needed it. Thank you again for helping me see God in everything. It makes every season of life, even if it's challenging, the greatest adventure there is."
—*Carrie Baller*

"You have truly spoken directly into my life. I, as a mother of five, found myself hanging on to your every word. As I go through my daily routines, your advice and wisdom echo in my mind."
—*April Doyle*

"I've been convinced that I must be doing something wrong; otherwise, my house would be in order, my kids wouldn't cry so much, and I wouldn't be so frustrated! Your book was just the answer I was looking for."
—*Deanna Sheffield*

"Your seven strategies have made a huge difference in the efficiency of my home, and as I apply them, I feel I am a better mother and wife."
—*Kim Henderson*

"With your tips and techniques, I have become more organized and calm about my life—kids, husband, and house included."
—*Lisa Wilinsky*

"I know it was God leading you to jump in feet first and launch your book, if for no other reason but to speak volumes to me."
—*Kathy Eddy*

"Your stories, your passion, and your humor are a special blessing…. I pray God will use your gift of words to inspire, encourage, and uplift moms all over the country."
—*Lori Stevens*

"I know *Coach Mom* will have a lasting impact on all who read it."
—*Kim Heaton*

COACH
MOM

COACH
MOM

7 STRATEGIES FOR
ORGANIZING YOUR FAMILY
INTO AN ALL-STAR TEAM

Brenna Stull (signature)

BRENNA STULL

Ps. 90:12

NEW HOPE
PUBLISHERS

Birmingham, Alabama

New Hope® Publishers
P. O. Box 12065
Birmingham, AL 35202-2065
www.newhopepublishers.com

Library of Congress Cataloging-in-Publication Data

Stull, Brenna, 1968-
Coach mom : 7 strategies for organizing your family into an all-star
team / Brenna Stull.
   p. cm.
Includes bibliographical references.
ISBN-13: 978-1-59669-022-6 (soft cover)
1. Mothers—Religious life. 2. Home—Religious aspects—Christianity.
I. Title.
BV4529.18.S78 2007
248.8'431—dc22
     2006026549

ISBN: 978-1-59669-022-6

N074125 • 0407 • 5M1

DEDICATION

This book is dedicated to my all-star team...
and one all-star in particular—Micah.

This sweet three-year-old patiently gave up his
time with me—an hour every morning for four
months—while I plinked out my first draft.

The writing of this book was our secret, only
to be known by the others after the first draft was
complete. Every morning while my husband, Chris,
was at work, Micah's older brothers were at school,
and his baby sister was napping, we made our way
to the computer keyboard. He contentedly and
quietly worked puzzles at my feet, zoomed cars
on the floor, and enjoyed Cheerios while I worked.
But my *most inspired* times of writing were the times
that he sat sweetly on my lap, with his arms and
legs wrapped around me and head leaning on my
chest near my heart.

TABLE OF CONTENTS

CHAPTER 3
STRATEGY: REMOVE AND APPROVE

CHAPTER 4
STRATEGY: HAVING A PLACE GIVES YOU SPACE

CHAPTER 5
STRATEGY: HAVE A NOTION ABOUT YOUR MOTION

ACKNOWLEDGMENTS

Thank you to...

Esther Burroughs, my inspiration, mentor, and advocate.

Tim Kimmel for your advice, wisdom, and encouragement.

New Hope Publishers for partnering with me to encourage moms.

Tamara Overton, my triplet sister and best friend. You have worn many hats, depending on the need: encourager, copy editor, and caring aunt.

Angie Bowsher, my good friend who wore the same three hats as my sister: encourager, copy editor, and caring "aunt."

Gil and Delia Comon for the use of your home when finishing my first draft.

My parents, Don and Gerrie Blackley, and my in-laws, Clarence and Pam Stull. You are the greatest. Your healthy marriages are a legacy and a gift of security to your children and grandchildren. Thank you for your faithful parenting and grandparenting.

First Baptist Church, McKinney, Texas, Women of the Word Wednesday morning class members. Your words of encouragement, ideas, and cheers have helped me finish getting this material into book form. It was my privilege to pour out to you, face-to-face, this message God laid on my heart.

Georgia Lessard and my writers critique group, Janice Byrd, Susan Ellingburg, and Joy Bradford, for their hours of diligent editing.

Friends who proofed and prayed, including **Lesley Bain, Debbi Bayes, Karen Boyce, Barbara Davidson, Anita Eddy, Susannah Gobler, Mary Ann Lackland, Kay Mercer, Michelle Nolan,**

Angie Mosher, Mindy Mosher, Valerie New, Jill Rhodes, Jennifer Richardson, Birgitte Santaella, Sharon Scow, LeAnn Somborn, and Dawna Wood.

My husband, Chris Stull, and our children, Dillon, Derek, Caleb, Micah, and Karis Joy. Thank you for sharing me with others as you allow me to speak and write.

Christ Jesus, my Lord: *"I thank Christ Jesus our Lord, who has given me strength, that he considered me faithful, appointing me to his service"* (1 Timothy 1:12).

MORE THAN A SURVIVOR

Do you value a peaceful, joyful, loving home in which each minute is spent in a way that really counts? We all know that managing a home while raising children and nurturing a marriage takes time and energy. Do you work outside the home? You'll need to conserve time and energy even more. Are you a single parent *and* work outside the home? You'll need to be a *master* of time and energy conservation and intentional living.

Many moms can claim only to be *survivors* in their homes when they have young children. Our hurried culture only compounds the chaos and feelings of defeat. Through prayerful trial and error, I've found some answers. This book explores seven key principles, or strategies, for developing your family into a smoothly functioning team, on which every member has a role and plays an important part. Each strategy has seven practical applications showing ways the principles can be applied in daily life. Application of the strategies will not only save you time and energy, but will also focus your time and energy on what is really important.

The seven strategies I've developed for organizing a family into an all-star team grew out of my dire need for help. (My husband will attest to that.) Our fourth son was a one-year-old at the time I began the pursuit of handling things in a more God-honoring way. I was inconveniencing others with my tardiness and spending too much time looking for lost items and papers. My own disorderliness was keeping me from focusing on demonstrating love to my family and others around me.

I realized how much other moms need these answers at the first conference I taught on home efficiency. I was teaching in a room with a maximum capacity of 50 people and had 30 copies of each session's handout. But more than 100 women squeezed into the small, stuffy room the first session... sitting on the floor, standing in the back, leaning in from the hall, not even wanting to leave when the hour was over. The scenario was repeated during each of the sessions that weekend. In the six years since that time, I have had the privilege of sharing these strategies with hundreds of other women and have had the joy of personally witnessing the transformation of many hearts, homes, and families.

Since you are reading this book, I have a hunch that *you* want to do more than survive. You want to make the most of this season with little ones; you want to be as effective and intentional as you can be, creating a warm and peaceful home, nurturing your children, and growing in your marriage and other meaningful relationships. I want to propose to you, the mom, that you are the coach of your home team. You set the pace and the tone, you cheer others toward their goals as you reach your own, and you give the pep talk at the end of a hard day when a team member is discouraged. *You* can move your team toward victory in every area of life by organizing your family into an all-star team.

Would you allow me, a veteran coach who is still on the playing field, to lead you through this playbook of strategies for moms? In the following chapters, we'll look at the day-to-day choices we can make as coaches of our families: what we fight to protect, what we decide to let go, when we must give our all, when we may hold back, and how we manage our time and all that is in our care.

Not Naturally Gifted

I've been teaching drawing lessons for 12 years. One thing that makes me a great art teacher is the fact that I'm not a natural artist. I wasn't a prodigy artist—sitting down as a kid to draw elaborate pictures of things. But my grandmother trained my eyes to look at things in a way that allowed me to reproduce them on paper. I can draw anything I can see.

I walk my students through drawing, step-by-step, and train their eyes in the same way that my grandmother trained mine. Every one of my students succeeds, because a person doesn't have to be naturally gifted to draw well.

In the same way, I'm just an ordinary mom. My IQ is not unusually high (though I'm surrounded by family and friends whose IQs are), and I'm not naturally an orderly and neat person. I have a hard time even remembering to close cabinet doors after I open them. When absorbed in a conversation with a friend, I frequently lose track of time and run late to my next appointment. My husband and I daily have to work through the challenges of what it takes for two people to live together. And our kids sometimes belch in public restaurants, break windows with baseballs, and talk back to us.

So you see, I have some shortcomings, but let me tell you one of my positive traits: I have the intense desire to make the most of whatever God gives me, whether that is time, talents, opportunities, resources, relationships,…or children! I had five children in less than nine years. Through trial and error and *much prayer,* I've learned some things that make family life with children run smoother. And though I was not looking for one more thing to add to my plate, I felt compelled by God to write this book.

Every mom's application of these strategies will be different— as different and unique as each individual God has created. Just as all of my students succeed in their own ways, you too, without having to be naturally gifted, can succeed in having a home life that runs peacefully and smoothly.

Mother of Five

I never imagined myself as the mother of five children. *No way.* I always thought we would have three children, and my husband, Chris, always thought we would have two. He says we were *both* right. Others didn't picture me as a mother of five either. I remember talking with my father-in-law just days before giving birth to my first child. "I still just can't imagine *you* as a mom," he said with a chuckle. Then one day, after we had just given my in-laws the news of my fifth pregnancy, my mother-in-law said, "Well, I've been telling everyone...if *anyone* can handle five children,..." and as a streak of pride shot through my veins, she finished her statement, "Chris can!"

To my surprise, I discovered having five children is truly a joy and a blessing, *and* I've learned to love and appreciate each growing stage. But with each stage, for each child, comes challenges...and the more children, the more numerous the challenges.

Efficiency—A Spiritual Issue

At first when I felt this growing passion for running the home in an efficient way, I wondered if the subject was somewhat shallow, and I needed validation that this was worth sharing with others. It just didn't seem as important as other more "spiritual" topics I'd pursued in the past, like prayer and Scripture memory. Then I realized this really is a *vital* part of my spiritual pilgrimage. My goal is to please God by living a life of love, and that takes intentional living.

I find it's hard to live a life of love when I'm already running behind schedule and can't find my car keys...or when I'm overwhelmed with my home and feel I'm the only one working to keep it going...or when I am frazzled and can't find time to pray...or when I am running from one self-imposed crisis to the next, feeling the guilt of overcommitment and not following through with jobs, leaving them half done...or when company is coming and a panic attack is beginning as I look at the disorder in my house. Yes, home management is *definitely* a spiritual issue.

The Crucial Element

We may believe that in marking our course with great resolution and having determination to stick with it, we can master our lives all on our own. But no matter how much we try, this life will never work well enough to create the peace and joy we long for deep inside. The Bible says, *"Obsession with self in these matters is a dead end; attention to God leads us out into the open, into a spacious, free life"* (Romans 8:6 *The Message*).

True freedom and peace in our hearts and homes start with trusting God and realizing that He is interested in every part of our daily life. The foundation for true effectiveness in the home is trusting God with our life and the lives of those in our home. A verse from the Bible that I've adopted as my life's verse is Psalm 90:12: *"Teach us to number our days aright, that we may gain a heart of wisdom."* I ask God daily to show me how to live in a way that pleases Him and makes the most of each moment He grants me. You can ask Him too—He always answers!

IT'S A DREAM TO HAVE A TEAM

JOB OPENING

Job Description

Long-term team players needed for challenging permanent work in an often chaotic environment. Candidates must possess excellent communication and organizational skills and be willing to work variable hours, including evenings, weekends, and frequent 24-hour shifts. Some overnight travel required, including trips to primitive camping sites on rainy weekends and sports tournaments. Travel expenses not reimbursed. Extensive courier duties also required. Length of employment: the rest of your life.

Responsibilities

Must be willing to face stimulating technical challenges, such as small gadget repair, mysteriously sluggish toilets, and stuck zippers. Must screen phone calls, maintain calendars, and coordinate production of multiple home-work projects. Must have ability to plan and organize social gatherings for clients of all ages and mental outlooks. Must handle assembly and product-safety testing of plastic toys and battery-operated devices. Must always hope for the best but be prepared for the worst. Responsibilities also include floor maintenance and janitorial work throughout the facility.

Possibility for Advancement and Promotion
Actually, none. Job is to remain in the same position for years, constantly retraining and updating your skills, so those in your charge can ultimately surpass you.

Previous Experience
No previous experience required. On-the-job training is offered on a continual basis.

Wages and Compensation
No wages. In fact, you pay those you supervise, offering frequent raises and bonuses. A balloon payment toward college is due when the child turns 18. And when you die, the child gets whatever is left.

Benefits
Although no health or dental insurance, no pension, no tuition reimbursement, no paid holidays, and no stock options are offered, this job supplies riches that money cannot provide.

Position
Mother, mom, mama, mommy

—Adapted from an email correspondence; author unknown

It takes courage to attempt to fill a job like that.

You have seen the news spots about moms on strike; these are women who have served their families to the point of burnout. They are worn out; they feel unappreciated and taken advantage of by the very ones they love the most.

I have had days that I wanted to place the "mom on strike" sign in my yard, go to bed, and pull the covers over my head.

How about you? Rather than focusing on those days, let's look at strategies for avoiding such days, so we can enjoy more often the benefits of motherhood—the riches that money cannot provide.

APPLICATION

1

Motivating Team Players

One of the ways we can avoid making the news in the midst of frustration is to involve our family in household jobs. Kathy Peel discusses the team concept in *The Family Manager:* It's a dream to have a team. If you have a baby, a one-year-old, and a two-year-old, I know this is hard to fathom. I remember one day I was talking with my sister, telling her some jobs my oldest had helped with around the house. At that point, my oldest was four years old. But Tamara had a two-year-old and a baby. She responded, "You mean children can be assets, not just liabilities?"

Yes, children do grow and mature—and as they do, it is our responsibility to teach them to do their part in helping the family. It seems children are eager to help with household chores...until they reach the age at which they really are able to help. But there are many ways that young children can effectively help in the home. It is our job as Coach Mom to train our players in these ways.

Practical Chore Motivators

Motivation, too, is one of the coach's primary responsibilities. As you train your team members to work effectively in the home, doing so will be easier if you use a variety of motivators. Explore different possibilities, and find out what works best for your team.

Motivator 1: Prize Basket. Provide your children an in-house "store" where they can go to spend the money earned from doing chores. Keep your prize basket stocked; prepurchase inexpensive items appropriate for their ages.

Workday prizes can go a long way in encouraging children to help. Letting them see the prizes *before* doing chores on a workday is highly motivating.

Children may also choose to put their toys in the prize basket with a price. When siblings shop and choose another sibling's item, they pay the owner. Though it recycles "stuff" through the house, it *is* cost-effective.

The prize basket does not help the decluttering process, but the benefits and fun it adds in keeping the house running smoothly usually outweigh that drawback.

After some time, donate remaining toys and prizes to teachers for classroom incentives, and restock the prize basket.

Motivator 2: Special Privilege. A great alternative to a workday prize is a workday special privilege. Assign values to desirable privileges, such as having a soda with dinner, staying up an hour later than usual, or having a friend over to play.

Motivator 3: Daily Assignments. By the age of three, most children are capable of helping with chores at home. Favorite daily assignments include emptying the dishwasher, gathering/ carrying out the trash, and sorting and delivering dirty laundry to the laundry room. Assign one household chore per family member daily.

Organizing Ideas for Chores

- **Daily chore chart:** Fashion this chart in a way that works for you. You might have one daily task chart that lists tasks for the day, such as making bed, brushing teeth, picking up toys, carrying out the trash. Or you might have a chart that lists all children's names and shows their chores for the day or week.
- **Chore drawing from bowl:** Have children draw chores out of a bowl and set the timer for when the chore should be completed. This works well if everyone is doing chores at the same time.
- **Initialing chore on completion:** List on erasable board the daily chores, and allow the children to place their

initials beside a chore when it is complete—first come, first served.

- **Musical chores:** Put on a CD, turn the volume up, and see who can get the most done before the music stops.
- **Quantify tasks:** For daily picking up, give the children specific tasks to make the job seem manageable. Say, "Put away seven things" instead of "Pick up your room."

Each child is different, but the following are some guidelines for what children, or the little team players, can typically do at certain ages.

Three-year-olds can generally do these chores:
- Dress self.
- Wipe up spills.
- Put dirty clothes in hamper.
- Pick up toys.
- Sort clean silverware (after washing hands).
- Make bed (using only a comforter).
- Help carry in light groceries.
- Put place mats, plastic plates, and utensils around the table.
- Fill water bottles.

Four-year-olds can do all of the previous chores and these:
- Help empty dishwasher.
- Feed pets.
- Gather and sort dirty laundry (in mesh fold-down bags).
- Match clean socks.
- Scrub vegetables.
- Fold towels and washcloths.
- Put away clothes in drawers.
- Pick up toys.
- Wipe bathroom sink and counter with premoistened cleaning wipes.
- Wipe windows with cleaning wipes for windows.

Five-year-olds can do all of the previous chores and these:
- Vacuum small areas with a lightweight, handheld vacuum.
- Sweep porch.
- Help empty wastebaskets.
- Dust furniture (feather duster or rag).
- Sort and straighten toys.
- Put clean clothes away neatly.
- Get mail and put it in the proper place.

Six-year-olds and older children can do all of the previous chores and these:
- Take out the garbage.
- Sweep stairs and walks.
- Clean out the car (using two sacks: one for throwaways and one for put-away items).
- Vacuum their own rooms.
- Empty the dishwasher.
- Sort clothes for washing.
- Organize own drawers and closet.
- Clean outdoor furniture.
- Water potted plants and garden.
- Set and clear the table.
- Make juice.
- Rake leaves.
- Help put groceries away.
- Pack own sack lunch (using premade sandwiches).

Motivator 4: Weekly Allowance. Pick a day to pay the children each an allowance for doing their daily chores consistently through the week. Saturday is an easy day to remember if you are laying out offering envelopes to take to church in the morning. It is a good reminder that we are to give a portion of our earnings back to the Lord.

Christian bookstores sell banks that have three slots (give, spend, and save) to teach children the principle of using money wisely. Giving 10 percent, saving 20 percent, and spending 70 percent is a good principle to teach.

Rosalyn, my friend and mother of four boys, checks her children's chore charts before handing out allowances. She has a place on each child's chore chart to record allowance deductions. Deductions are given for complaining, talking back, fighting, and more. She allows them only one warning before a deduction is taken.

Motivator 5: Fun. Make it fun. Say, "Everyone pick up seven things as fast as you can!" or "Everyone pick up anything with red or yellow on it." For tough jobs that are above and beyond the regular daily chores, dispense one "energy pill" per minute the timer is set. Energy pills can be anything small—yogurt-covered raisins, chocolate chips, or some small candy.

Motivator 6: "Carrots." When guiding children throughout the day, have them do the less-desirable tasks—such as chores, homework, or practicing piano—before allowing them to do the more desirable things (carrots)—such as playing with a neighborhood friend or getting out a toy. Flip-flopping this routine often leads to frustration.

Motivator 7: Mother's Helper. Hire a mother's helper. The willing seven- to nine-year-old sibling or neighbor can entertain your toddler on-site while you get things done. Two to three dollars an hour is the going rate.

Put Players in Positions to Succeed

In the summertime when my older children are home and I need help with the little ones, I first check with them to see if they would like the job.

My playful son, Derek, loves children. One Saturday morning, we were at the ball fields early for Caleb's baseball game. Because Dillon and Derek had a game immediately following Caleb's game, they wore their uniforms. About 15 minutes into Caleb's game, I looked over at the playground area beside the field, and there was my Derek (a.k.a. the Pied Piper) with all the preschool siblings gathered around him. He was building castles and moats and telling stories—he had them captivated. His white pants were covered in brown dirt, and he was filling his moats with the cold water from the only water bottle I packed for him for the hot Phoenix morning! At age eight, Derek may not have been interested in a two-hour cleaning expedition with his mom, but he was the perfect candidate to be hired to entertain his one-year-old sister and three-year-old brother while I did some kid-free cleaning. *Coach Mom's checkoff: player in the right position.*

What about your husband? He most likely is willing to consider what his part might be for helping in the home. On a date night or during some other unhurried, low-stress, noncrisis time, sit down and talk about it. Tell him the things you appreciate about what he is currently doing in his job and at home. Express to him how you feel. Keeping emotions at bay, present a plan to him in a rational way, and ask if he is willing to buy into it.

Involve your whole family—including the children, as soon as they are able—in household tasks; this will be best not only for you but for each family member too. Delegating some of the daily simple tasks will give you more energy to focus on the more demanding aspects of home management. In one day, moms do everything from wiping up what the sick child left on the floor to trying to wipe out unkind words of siblings; from repairing broken remote-control cars to repairing children's broken hearts; from cleaning up a potty trainee's dirty underwear to cleaning up what is left of a child's confidence after a public demeaning by a coach.

It's a heavy load. When possible, share it. Remember: It's a dream to have a team.

WHAT NOW, COACH?

- List four daily chores that you would like to delegate.
- List children's names and household chores they could possibly do.
- Identify a chore you would like to ask your husband to cover.

2

Respected and Understood

A major aspect of team building has to do with each family member feeling respected and understood. That goes for the three-foot-tall family members as well as the six-foot-tall ones. Preschoolers can be difficult to understand—of course, so can anyone. **Seek to understand each of your children.**

Study Personalities

Study your children to see what makes them tick. I used to wonder if my three-year-old firstborn sat in his room thinking up schemes to drive me crazy. For example, he was adamant about having his shoes tied "just right." He went through a phase during which I tied his shoes a dozen times in a row before the results were to his liking.

I finally figured out that he is a detail person (the opposite of his mother), and the way his shoes were tied really was important to him. I decided to put my efforts into teaching *him* to tie his shoes so he could make them "just right" himself. It often took him a dozen times, but he was happy to do it to reach his desired outcome. (Side note: Investing time in teaching children to tie shoes and pump themselves on swings at an early age pays great dividends.)

Identify Their Feelings

Communicate. Repeat back to your children what you hear them saying. We must learn to identify with their feelings, then redirect them. Repeating back to them what they are saying calms their emotions—they feel understood. After that, they are better prepared to be directed. With toddlers, after acknowledging their feelings, distraction or redirection is effective.

It is important to validate their feelings even when the feelings do not reflect reality. For example, apply that colorful bandage to the "terrible" hurt and give a hug and a kiss, even though you know that what your child actually needs the most is just some personal attention from Mama. My three-year-old still believes that Mama's kisses instantly heal all scrapes and cuts, and I'm cherishing every last kissing opportunity.

Older children need to be understood too. We made an interesting discovery when our two oldest sons were eight and seven years old. We had recently moved, and the four boys were separated, being assigned to one of two rooms. I had considered splitting up the two oldest boys, Dillon and Derek, as they are at opposite ends of the scale in orderliness. But after considering several factors, such as they wore the same size clothes, their bedtime was later than the younger boys', the computer and desk were in the room allotted to the big boys, and that room was bigger, I decided it was best to keep them together. I felt it was a good decision.

A year later, Dillon's social studies All About Me packet came home. I was a bit surprised by Dillon's completion of the sentence, "The thing I fear the most is. . . ." The terrorist attacks of September 11 had just happened, and I thought he might mention something about world security. No, he did not. He had written, "sharing a room with Derek." And this was not the only place he mentioned this issue in his report.

As soon as I had a moment for the two of us to sit down and talk, I told him that I had read his comments. "*This* is something I can do something about," I said.

"I'm just tired of picking up after him all the time," he said.

"The only option I can see," I said, "is if you are willing to move into the other bedroom, which means sharing with your three-year-old brother a smaller room without a computer or desk."

He started jumping up and down, saying, "Yes! Yes! When can we do it?"

Even though Dillon seemed glad and relieved and the initial responses from my other boys were very positive (Derek was excited to move to the top bunk, and my five-year-old was thrilled to move up to the bigger high-tech room), I still had my doubts about this. I would not let Dillon move his clothes until after a one-week trial.

However, it worked out beautifully, as my first and fourth sons lean toward the Tidy Tim tendency. Also, once Derek had his clothes in drawers to himself and he did not have his older brother looking over his shoulder, he stepped it up a notch on the orderliness scale.

I am thankful that we found out about Dillon's life frustration and were able to make a change. I pray that we will stay connected enough with our children to know how they feel about things.

Stay in Touch

"What's your beef?" family dinners: Parenting expert Tim Kimmel suggests having nights when the children decide on the dinner menu and are encouraged to share their concerns. As the family gathers around the dinner table, the children express their feelings about family situations. The one rule is that Mom and Dad are not allowed to justify situations or be defensive in any way. They may only listen and try to understand where each child is coming from.

Puppet interviews during family dinner: Interview one family member during the family dinner. Provide a puppet for that family member to use in answering questions. Children will often express through a puppet thoughts or emotions that they would not make known otherwise. Start with lighter subjects, such as favorite foods, books, and activities, then move to deeper subjects, such as what they have been disappointed in, what they would change, fears, hopes, and dreams.

 WHAT NOW, COACH?

- Work on really *listening* to your children this week. In difficult moments, look them in the eyes and repeat back to them your understanding of what they said. This will help your children feel important and valued.
- Record what you learn from these listening experiences.

APPLICATION

3

Power-Packed Words

I stomp into the room, glare at the lazy couch potatoes still sitting in their pajamas at 10:30 A.M. on a Saturday morning, and start barking out commands: "Your rooms are a mess! We will first bring those to complete order." The family room is a mix of pillows and sleeping bags. "Up and at it...*NOW!*"

At moments like this, I find myself wondering, *Why isn't anyone hopping to get the chores done? Why does everyone have such bad attitudes?*

I need look no further than the mirror to understand why. I know that, as Coach Mom, I am setting the tone for the whole team, and it is not a good one. A few times, I have had to stop, pray, and then do a "take two" in approaching my family for help.

Take two might go like this:

- Smile and say, "Good morning." Give hugs.
- Give a notice that we will be changing gears in X number of minutes, considering the minutes left in a program or game, if possible.
- Explain the strategy for tackling housecleaning.
- Mention that this is not an optional activity, but everyone who is extra diligent and has a good attitude through it all will earn extra money or some other reward.

> *A word aptly spoken is like apples of gold*
> *in settings of silver.*
> —Proverbs 25:11

Quick Start

Boys really get into the good-overcoming-evil theme! If you have boys, you might let them pick out a superhero costume to wear during the cleaning session and then say: "Look around you at how bad things are. Do you think this mess can prevail against an awesome team like us? No way!" Remind them of the extra rewards and incentives along the way and that rewards are given only when tasks are done quickly and with a good attitude.

Reinforce the facts that they are each a vital part of the team and that the job cannot be done without them. (Lord knows it can't!) Then *praise, praise, praise* them for doing their part. Make light of work; then allow time to enjoy each other when it is done.

Weighty Words, Praise Words

It is easy to bring to children's attention the negative things they are doing rather than the positive things. Yet it is imperative for them to hear positive things from us.

As Chris addresses our boys throughout the day, I hear one word repeated over and over: champ. "Let's get ready and go, champ." "Champ, how was your day?" "Go brush your teeth, champ." Words like that build up a spirit.

Try not to respond to bad actions with bad child statements, such as, "You are such a bad boy." Instead, address the action. "That was a bad thing to do. You are a good boy, but you made a bad choice. I know you can do better next time."

Avoid comparing your children with their siblings. Express your appreciation for each one's unique traits, talents, and characteristics.

One of my boys has been struggling with the issue of kindness toward his younger brother this year. (Actually, each of them sometimes struggles with being kind toward the next younger sibling.) As we have been talking about and praying about him showing more kindness, I have tried to take notice of the smallest positive act toward his brother, such as helping him work a puzzle, letting him play with his new toy, or pushing him on the swing; then I praise him saying, "I caught you being kind."

Hearing positive words directed toward others can also motivate children sometimes. One day when I said, "Let's all pick up 12 things!" and we were scurrying around, Caleb ran up to me and said, "I picked up 19 things!" He went above and beyond my expectations, so I said, "You were an 'extra-miler' today, Caleb!" Since then, many other extra-milers have been commended.

Another day, I made a point to brag on Micah for making his bed before I asked him to do it. The next morning, Caleb was up early and had made not only his bed but all of his brothers' beds also. Words are powerful.

Husbands Love Praise Too

Our husbands also draw strength from our words. Respect is the best gift we can give to our husbands (Ephesians 5:22, 33*b*).

- Compliment him in front of others.
- Talk (brag) about him behind his back to your mom.
- Tell your children how hard he works, and support him when he leads.
- Do not publicly correct your husband unless serious consequences will arise if you don't.
- Daily verbalize specific things you appreciate about him.
- Start an admiration journal for him.

I have a journal I use to jot down moments and situations in which I particularly admired my husband. On Valentine's Day each year, I put a ribbon around the journal and *re*give it to him so he can catch up on the latest admiration entries since last year. It's not only meaningful—it's cost-effective.

When we encourage our family by citing specific admirable acts and qualities about them, we are building courage into them and instilling them with strength to make more good decisions in the future. Build up your team members with your words.

 WHAT NOW, COACH?

- Look for opportunities to praise your children this week:
  - ✓ Praise your children for demonstrating specific character qualities (for example, honesty, diligence, and generosity).

✓ When one makes a wrong choice, say, "That was a bad thing to do. You are a good boy/girl, but you made a bad choice. You are better than that, and I know you will do better next time."

✓ Make a treat jar for your family. Use it to reward your children for good behavior.

• Look for opportunities to sincerely praise your husband this week:

✓ Say, "I really admire the way you _____ [state something specific he does or a character quality he demonstrates]."

✓ Compliment him in front of others.

✓ "Talk about him behind his back" (brag to others about him).

4

Getting Back to the Family Dinner

Which of the following do you think is most important to child development?

A. School

B. Playtime

C. The family dinner

D. Storytime

Catherine Snow, professor of education at Harvard Graduate School of Education, studied 65 families over an eight-year period. She found that dinnertime was of more value to child development than playtime, school, and storytime. We will drive across town two times a day, five days a week, to put our children in the best school. But are we willing to take the time to plan a family dinner each night?

"But It's Too Much Work!"

The hour just before dinner is a great time to develop a bad attitude. Just ask my children...or me, for that matter. I am not one who gets a thrill out of the process of preparing meals.

If you have small children, you do not have endless hours to look at recipe books and set just the perfect table every day—even if you *do* enjoy cooking. And even Miss Hospitality can get out of sorts when she feels like she is the only one doing the work that goes into a family dinner: preparing the food, setting the table, filling drinks, clearing the table, wiping countertops, and washing dishes. But we need to commit to having family dinners, so line up some help, keep it simple, be creative, and have some fun.

It's a wonderful dream to have a team in the dinner arena. Would you like some hints that can help you make it happen?

Assign kitchen patrol duty (KP). Assign one child per day to be on duty. The person on KP

- ✓ sets the table, being creative if inspired (stuffed animal centerpieces are fine);
- ✓ decides who sits where (unless the family enjoys the predictability of assigned seats);
- ✓ delivers things needed during dinner (refills on drinks, salt and pepper, an extra utensil, or extra napkins);
- ✓ receives an encouraging word and thanks from each family member;
- ✓ clears the table afterwards;
- ✓ does not grumble or complain, knowing that grumbling is actually volunteering to be on KP for the next dinner!

Make family dinner a priority. Something happens when we sit down facing each other (instead of the television) at the table and "break bread" together. Connection is made. And this practice sends a message to our children about the importance of time together and the value of our relationships.

Family dinners are difficult to keep up regularly, especially when children grow old enough to be involved in evening practices and activities. But it is a healthy goal to try to sit together at the dinner table at least four nights a week. If you can't pull that off, you might need to take it as a sign of overcommitment and drop a few things.

Adjust expectations and keep it simple. Lighten up and let go of some expectations. Make meals simple, and serve them with love—even when using paper and plastic. Your goal is time together. Lots of seemingly normal dinners add up to hours of accrued quality time together through the years.

- Find out what simple meals your family likes: build-your-own sandwiches; raw vegetables, boiled eggs, cheese and crackers, and fruit.
- Pick up a rotisserie chicken or some other prepared food on your way home from work or other activity. Who cooks the food is not what matters; taking the time to sit and eat together is what matters.
- Keep paper plates and plastic cups on hand for when schedule is tight.

Be creative. If you get in late from work, if you or your husband work odd hours, if you are a single parent working a long shift, or if you have team practices to work around, extra creativity will be required to plan and pull off the family dinner. Depending on your circumstances, consider these options:

- Provide an early nutritious snack for the children; then have a late dinner together.
- Let the children eat dinner and bathe; then sit together later at the family dinner table to eat dessert.
- Eat an early family dinner together, and then allow the children a healthy snack before going to bed.
- Utilize the slow cooker to have meals ready when you arrive home.

Focus family celebrations around dinnertime. Use a "You are special today!" plate at dinner to honor a family member for a special occasion or accomplishment: birthday, graduation, outstanding grade, act of honor or courage, dramatic exhibition of a positive character quality,...even potty-training success. The possibilities are endless.

Either purchase an official "You are special today!" plate or just use a plate that is different from the everyday plates and make it known to the family that this is the designated special plate. Special meanings can be attached also to one-of-a-kind cups, place mats, or whatever items you choose.

Make sure each family member is getting the daily nutrition needed. The family dinner feeds both body *and* spirit.

 ## WHAT NOW, COACH?

- Have dinner as a family at least four nights this week. And allow no television watching during dinner!
- Try the puppet interview during a family dinner.
- Write down a "question for the night"; then let all family members answer it at a family dinner this week.

APPLICATION
5

Dealing with Disobedience

A recurring sickness affects home life from time to time. If you have young children, you undoubtedly have it flare up at least once a day. What's the name of this sickness? Disobedience. I have been battling this disease in my children for ten years, and my parents battled the same disease in me.

I wish that 1,000 milligrams of vitamin C daily would make it go away. Unfortunately, it isn't cured that easily. However, there are some steps you can take that do wonders in raising your home's immunity to this sickness. Administer **clear rules and** consequences, consistency, and constant affirmation daily to all children, and wash these down with a big dose of love and grace.

Establish clear rules and consequences. Take the time to instruct your children on what is right and wrong, what you expect them to do, and what will happen if they do not obey. This is especially important to remember to do when you are entering into a new situation, such as going to a restaurant or a wedding. Here are a couple of good rules for starters:

- Children get nothing that they cry for.
- From the time they are able to speak, children must politely use words (not grunts) to ask for things they want.

Select a consequence that *matters*. What makes your children tick? What do they consider important? What are their dreams? Make sure the consequences of a poor decision matter to the child who made that decision. For the child who treasures social interaction, consider taking away time with friends. An introverted child may respond best to a time-out. For the eager-to-please child, choose appropriate words to share clear and simple displeasure. Whatever is important to the child is your optimum teaching tool.

Oftentimes, simple acts can get your point across. My friend Jodi's preteen daughter recently slammed her door in a huff. Jodi simply hammered the pegs from the hinge and removed the door for a while.

> *Train a child in the way he should go,*
> *and when he is old he will not turn from it.*
> —Proverbs 22:6

Be consistent. Consistency is difficult because it takes such effort. It's easier to let things slide. "Teach from your feet, not your seat," I once heard someone say. Every time I get lazy and do not follow through with consequences for wrong actions, I regret it. It costs me! It is like taking one step forward, then three steps back. The more children I have had, the more steps back I've taken each time I have not followed through. Children are always observing and taking note for *their* future behavioral decisions. Effort today is "paying forward" to your children's maturity and your peace of mind.

Consistent, loving discipline is a way of showing your children love and respect. We tell our children that although we do not enjoy administering consequences to them, the Lord has given us the responsibility to teach them to make right choices.

Always be careful what you say, because you must follow through when your children don't meet expectations. On the other hand, be careful of promises also, because you must keep them.

Deal with problems swiftly and without anger. When I do not deal with a problem swiftly, it affects my relationship with the children. If I am not consistent with my discipline, it can build dissension between them; it also can build up in me resentment toward them, and then I explode when the same wrong action is repeated.

On the other hand, when I deal with the issue swiftly and administer the consequences privately, I am free to love without reserve. There is no need for a score sheet. I try to communicate to the offender that although I may not like that child's actions, I will always love him or her unconditionally. Thankfully, that is the way God treats me.

If necessary, give yourself time to cool down until you are able to discipline matter-of-factly. When my strong-willed preschoolers are throwing fits, I have to take a deep breath and pray for my own self-control. I try to say, "I am sorry you are upset that [insert whatever the issue is], but throwing a fit in the family room is unacceptable. You may move to your bedroom and close the door until you are finished."

Sometimes I have to physically pick up a child (arms and legs still flailing) and place that child in his or her bed, closing the door behind me.

It amazes me how a child can be fiery mad about something, then, after five to seven minutes of screaming and crying in his or her room, come back to the family room with a smile and say, "I'm finished," and move on to the next activity.

Teach your children to admit their faults. Susannah Wesley, mother of nineteenth-century pastor John Wesley, said when children freely confess their faults, they should not be punished; this rewards their honesty. On the other hand, she said never let a rebellious, sinful act go unnoticed.

Teach your children to say, "I was wrong," after they disobey. These are important words for all of us to be able to say, and the earlier they start (as soon as they can say words), the easier it will be.

When wrong, our children are led to say this prayer: "Dear God, I was wrong for what I did. Please help me to do better." This helps them realize they are answering to a higher authority. I remind them God is watching, even when Mommy isn't. And I remind them that God isn't finished with me yet either: Every day I have to pray and admit to God my shortcomings.

Constantly affirm your children. When your children have made poor or wrong decisions, hug them tightly and express your unconditional love and the confidence that they will make better decisions in the future. Then be on the lookout for better decisions. Praise your children with statements specific to the circumstances: "I caught you being kind to your sister." "You kept a happy heart and quickly obeyed when Mommy said it was time to leave your friend's house." Your words and even the smallest of rewards, such as the special plate at dinnertime or a happy heart certificate, go a long way in reinforcing good decisions.

Once Dillon received a wand as a birthday gift; at the top of the wand was a star filled with hundreds of tiny star candies. "Can we have some star candies, Mom?" I would hear Dillon and four-year-old Derek ask every day for weeks.

"You may have ten each," I would sometimes say.

"OK!" They would happily cheer as they counted out their tiny stars.

As the weeks went on, I cut the numbers every now and then. "You may have three today, boys."

"OK!" they answered, and were quickly off to play after their treat. I was impressed with their compliance and contentment.

Finally, one day (weeks after Dillon's birthday and only about halfway into the star candies), the daily question was asked again: "Can we have some star candies, Mom?"

I looked into their eager eyes, feeling deep in my heart that even if I said, "You may have one each," that I would not hear complaints. "Take them *all*, boys. Take them *all*."

"What? Whoa-hoa!"

I reveled in seeing the excitement with which they poured out all the stars on the counter and began dividing them up and popping them in their little mouths. At that moment, I felt my heavenly Father breathe a silent word to my heart: *That's what I enjoy doing for you. When I know that no matter what I say, your answer will always be, without a shadow of a doubt, "OK," that frees Me to bless you in the ways I desire, My daughter.*

The Great Physician offers me clear rules and consequences, consistency, and constant affirmation…with overflowing love and grace. Those are key factors in building team health, morale, and success. I pray I will walk daily in obedience, lovingly and wisely teaching my all-stars to do the same.

 ## WHAT NOW, COACH?

- List areas in which your children are struggling to make good choices. Communicate to your children the rules and expectations related to these areas. Also communicate the consequences of not meeting those expectations.
- When the children disobey, work on disciplining them *unemotionally*. Record one instance when you did this.
- Implement a reward system to reward your children for good behavior.

APPLICATION

6

Individual Interactions

Pastor John Wesley's mother, Susannah, mother to 17 children, spent an hour every day praying for her children. But she did not leave it at that. She made an investment of time in each of their lives. She spent one hour alone each week with each of her children, instructing them in spiritual matters.

When my oldest was nine, I began to get more intentional about my individual time with my children. My goal was to spend 20 minutes of time alone with each child each week. I wanted to start with a small achievable goal and work up from there, but I found that even 20 minutes a week was a challenge. That showed me how little individual attention I had been giving to them.

We can buy our children many things, but as much as we might be tempted on a busy week to look for a *buytimewithmychild.com* Web site, no one can sell that special time to us. We must plan and then stop what we are doing long enough to have meaningful interactions with each of our children. It builds them up, enriches the parent-child relationship, and helps us understand them better.

Here are some do's and don'ts for individual interaction time with your children:

Do's (This list is great for daddies to use too.)
- Calendar the time for individual interaction, or you will always put it off until the next week. (If you have a baby, it is wise to plan for interaction time with the older children during the baby's naptime.)
- Let the children decide the activity for their individual time. For little ones, you may want to give them two or three options to choose from.
- It does not have to cost any money, but it does cost *time*, which is the greatest gift you can give your children.

- Allow only true emergencies to interrupt the time you have set aside.
- Set the timer for the allotted time, and let the other children know you are off-limits during that time. They will honor that rule for each other, since they know the others will honor it when their time comes.

Don'ts
- Do not try to pull a "two for one" with this activity to accomplish something you need done. (I tried it, and it does not work.) This special time is all about the child.
- Do not make an effort to get quality time with all your children at once. Play with them individually, even if you just start with 10 minutes a week.

In between individual times, be playful with them all. Spice up your group times with lots of fun. I have always loved to sing and dance with my children. I make up silly songs about whatever we are doing; that makes them giggle until their tummy muscles hurt. This playfulness comes naturally when I am spending time alone with the Lord and allowing Him to refill my spiritual and emotional cup. The joy spills over and sometimes I just can't contain it.

Build up your children with *time*, and you will have loyal and happy team players.

 ## WHAT NOW, COACH?

- Calendar 20 minutes of time alone with each of your children this week. Let each child decide what you will do together for 20 minutes. List your children's names and the activity you did together. Record anything new you learned about your children during their individual times.
- Calendar a date with your husband, schedule a babysitter, and then enjoy.

7

Allowing a Voice, Giving a Choice

Another important factor in team building is allowing team members to make age-appropriate choices. These days, parents are giving their children more choices than ever before. Two-year-olds are deciding on bedtimes, the time they are willing to leave a play date, and what extra items will be bought from the grocery store (*or else*). It is not right. But you will rarely find a two-year-old who isn't *trying* to do all those things!

One good rule to employ is that the children will not get a choice in any matters in which they whine, cry, or throw a fit. Enforce that rule, and whining and crying in your home will take a nosedive.

Choices Within Boundaries

How can we allow our children to make choices within our boundaries? Try offering them multiple choices like these:

- "Would you like to read *Goodnight Moon* or *The Very Hungry Caterpillar*?" It is good to give the choice of two to three books rather than the whole bookcase, as a preschooler can easily get overwhelmed by too many options.
- "Would you like to eat your carrots cooked or raw?"
- "Do you want to pick up your toys before or after you brush your teeth?"
- "Would you like to practice piano before or after breakfast?"

There are all kinds of ways we can accomplish what needs to be done and still allow our children a voice.

One Saturday, I made an announcement in the family room at 12:30 P.M.: "We will have room cleanup at 1:00 P.M. Anyone whose room is already clean does not have to participate." The children scurried to their rooms to get started. By about 12:50 P.M., most were back in the family room with smug smiles on their faces.

At 1:00 P.M. when my timer rang, I said, "OK, it's time for room cleanup."

"We don't have to do it. Our rooms are already clean!" they said.

They were pleased because they did not have to participate in Mom's cleanup, and I was pleased that we reached the desired end...early.

Another evening, we were driving home from tennis lessons when someone remembered the fact that we would be passing our favorite pizza place. "We want pizza! We want pizza!" they all began chanting. I said, "Guys, I have a roast in the slow cooker. It will be ready for us when we get home. We are not stopping for pizza."

As they continued to implore, I realized we were not getting beyond the issue and it needed to be resolved, so I said, "I have roast you can eat for free. But if you want pizza and are willing to pay for it, I will stop."

Silence. Then I heard a few conversations about who wanted to pool a dollar or two each.

Amazingly, when we passed the pizza place, everyone agreed that roast sounded delicious. The ball was in their court, and they made the choice.

Sleeping Choices

We need to look for ways to meet the needs of the hearts of our children, as revealed by their requests; these ways must be suitable for both the parents and the children. Requests about sleeping times and locations are sometimes representative of heart needs.

It is our experience that two-year-olds often get up in the middle of the night and try to crawl in bed with their parents. Without having to share your bed and interrupt your sleep, you can make some arrangements that give the child the security of being near you. Allow children to sleep on the floor beside the bed if they come in during the night. Keep a blanket and small pillow handy for them to sleep on. My friend Chae tells her children they are allowed to come sleep on the floor in the parents' room as long as they get the blanket and pillow themselves and lie down without waking up the parents.

With our first son, we were very strict, telling him he needed to do certain things because those were the rules. With our last three children, we have been better about giving options from an early age. With some encouragement from parenting expert and author Tim Kimmel, we began allowing our children more choices, telling them that as long as they stayed within our bounds, they could have their way.

For a few weeks when Micah was three years old, he wanted to sleep at night almost anywhere but his bed. One night he asked to sleep on the couch in the living room.

With our firstborn, we probably would have said, "A bed is where we sleep at night, and we have one specifically for you. Think of all the children in the world who do not have a bed. Let's pray and thank God for providing you this comfortable bed to sleep in."

To Micah's request, we instead said, "As long as you will keep your eyes shut, lie still, and stay there all night, we will allow it." We spread his sleeping bag out, and he grabbed a pillow, curled up in the sleeping bag, and immediately went to sleep. He stayed there all night.

Another night he asked to sleep there again, but Dillon was still up doing homework at the living room table, so we were not sure if he would be able to sleep with the light on and the temptation to talk to Dillon. Yet we decided to let him give it a try. "Since you did so well last time, we will allow it. But if you talk, open your eyes, or move around, we will need to move you to your bed," we said. Again, he happily curled up and fell asleep.

The following weeks, he slept on the floor of his bedroom, on the floor of his brothers' bedroom, on the couch in the family room, and back in his own bed—he was all over. He stayed within the set boundaries, and I believe he felt some level of satisfaction in making some decisions for his own life.

Naptime can be a battle with preschoolers, but it is well worth defending for years. Instead of taking a "you *have* to sleep" approach at naptime, tell them that they do not have to go to sleep; they just have to lie still with their eyes closed for a half hour.

Giving children a voice in the family goes a long way in team building. And it's a dream to have a team.

 ## WHAT NOW, COACH?

- Say no to everything that a child whines or cries for.
- Allow your children to make some choices for themselves, as long as those choices do not hinder the accomplishment of the things that need to get done.
- List your children's names and write by their names at least one age-appropriate choice you allowed them to make this week.

THINK THROUGH BEFORE YOU DO

Before diving into a project or even into daily life, take the time to plan—you must think through before you do.

I heard of a man who hopped into his car one day and took off driving, with his wife by his side. When questioned by his wife about going the wrong direction, he replied, "I was making such good time I hated to turn around." How many times are we zooming through life without our final destination in mind?

One important part of thinking through before you do involves pausing long enough to think about your purpose and goals. It takes planning to move purposely through each day and not get caught up in the tyranny of the urgent.

APPLICATION

What's Your Game Plan?

Have you taken the time to think about what your family is all about? What do you most value? What is most important in your life? The process of writing a family purpose statement and establishing personal and family goals will help you and your husband clarify your purpose as a family. As you navigate your family through life, it will serve as a compass.

> *Family purpose determines family goals;*
> *family goals determine family schedule.*

Write a Family Purpose Statement

Dan Yeary, our pastor when we lived in Phoenix, encourages every family to have its own mission statement that acts as the foundation supporting each of the family's specific goals. Here's the Stull family's purpose: "To grow in our relationship with God and please Him through (1) our marriage, (2) our family, and (3) extending love to people." The family purpose statement dictates our goals, and our goals dictate our schedule.

Set Personal Goals Yearly

If you want to live an intentional life, take the time to set specific and measurable personal goals each year in multiple categories: physical, emotional, spiritual, and mental. This goal-setting time is a great time to sit down with your spouse to assess the past year and discuss your roles and expectations of each other. Set goals that support your family purpose statement. Keep the goals in a place where you will see them on a daily basis throughout the year.

Examples of Personal Goals
- **Physical goal:** Exercise for 30 minutes or more at least four times a week.
- **Emotional goal:** Schedule quality time with a friend at least two times a month.
- **Spiritual goal:** Read through the one-year Bible this year. (With one-year Bibles, a person can read through the entire Bible in one year simply by reading the text under each day's date throughout one year.)

- **Mental goal:** Read at least six books (not including the Dr. Seuss and Eric Carle libraries).

It's important that mothers of little ones continue to grow and be challenged mentally. Stay-at-home moms especially must be intentional about personal growth, since most of the daily hours are spent dealing with monotonous tasks of cleaning, changing diapers, feeding babies, carpooling, and folding clothes. All too often, I see a fresh, living spring full of hope become a stagnant cesspool that threatens to dry up completely if a conscious choice is not made to move ahead and focus on the beautiful terrain down the way.

Are you wondering how you can possibly set goals, much less reach them, during this physically demanding season? I have heard it said that people should not set goals that depend on someone else, or disappointment is bound to come, as others can block their goals at no fault to themselves. If a mom goes by that rule, she might not set any goals for 10, 15, or even 20 years. Moms all have dependents. Another option for moms is to set goals, but be flexible and strive to keep realistic expectations. Let's face it—something simple like an outbreak of chicken pox in a family can drastically alter family plans for over a month.

Set Personal Long-Term Goals

Solomon, known for his wisdom, said, *"There is a time for everything, and a season for every activity under heaven"* (Ecclesiastes 3:1). Family expert Tim Kimmel refers to this wisdom with a slight revision: "There is a time for everything, but not time for everything."

Writing down long-term goals can keep dreams alive for even the most sleep-deprived and overwhelmed mom, as they encourage her, reminding her that this physically demanding season will not last forever. The hope of seasons to come can be a glimmer of light shining in a dark night.

I have goals that are on hold as I am involved in full-time service to my family. Someday I'm going to be a *great* tennis player. My current tennis workout amounts to strapping two preschoolers into car seats so we can take their older brothers to their tennis lessons. Long-term goals give me perspective on the seasons of life, and I realize it's OK to put some dreams on the shelf for this season.

Set Family Goals

The final step in setting goals that support your purpose statement is setting family goals. Included in this list will be specific and measurable goals for the entire family as well as goals that center on marriage building. Consider the following as possible goals.

Examples of Family-Building Goals

- Sitting down for dinner together as a family five nights a week to connect. (See chapter 1 for details on the benefits and how-tos of pulling off the family dinner.)
- Read a book or book series together as a family. The key to success with this goal is to put the toddler to bed beforehand.

Examples of Marriage-Building Goals

- Regular date nights
- Getaway weekends

The best gift we can give our children is a strong and secure marriage. Plan a date with hubby—an intentional place to connect—each week or every two weeks. Are you on a tight budget? Trade babysitting with friends, and have a picnic in the park.

If you are looking for a good investment—the one that will give you the most bang for your buck—I've got the answer! Getaway weekends can be the best investment of time and money that you can make for your marriage. Simple is great. The goal is time together: stay overnight at an in-town hotel, eat out or take a picnic to a park, and stroll around a nice shopping center. If you get away every six months, you might notice a trend. For the first three months after your getaway, you will be carried through the tough times by looking back at the great time you just enjoyed.

And for the next three months, the anticipation of the next planned weekend will see you through.

If you are a single mom, you will need a getaway weekend all the more. With the added pressures of managing a home, children, and job single-handedly, you must take time to stop and rejuvenate. Look to your extended family or church community for help. Perhaps your sons could go on a men's ministry camping trip with a trusted friend and positive male role model. Or Grandpa and Grandma could take the children for a special weekend while you have a girls' overnight at a local hotel.

Finding care for the children is rarely easy. During our first ten years of parenthood, we, like many, lived 1,000 miles away from our parents. One year we spent an hour and a half at the beginning and end of our getaway just dropping off and picking up children from the various homes where they stayed. And when a friend recently kept our children here in our own home, I left six pages of single-spaced instructions/explanations. Yes, it *was* worth it.

Compass? Check!

Don't consider going any further in your family's journey without your compass: your family purpose statement. Let your goals be your map, and may your schedules bring you closer each day to each other and to your desired destination.

 WHAT NOW, COACH?

- Plan a time to write your family purpose statement. Post the time in the calendar; then do it.
- Set and record goals:
    - ❑ Yearly personal goals: physical, emotional, spiritual, and mental
    - ❑ Family goals and marriage goals
    - ❑ Long-term goals (personal and/or family goals)

APPLICATION

9

What Plays Are You Running?

> *Don't act thoughtlessly, but try to understand*
> *what the Lord wants you to do.*
> —Ephesians 5:17 (NLT)

A recurring theme in this book is making each moment count. This *does not* refer to packing every minute with activity, moving faster, and adding more to your schedule. It *does* refer to doing the right thing at the right time in the right way.

Making Intentional Scheduling Choices

Thinking through before you do is important when deciding to what activities your family will commit. Psychologist Phil McGraw says the problem is that most of our choices are motivated by what we *don't* want instead of by what we want. Here are a few examples of fear-based decisions:

- I don't want the kids to get behind others athletically, so I will overextend our commitments to put them on both teams again.
- I don't want the principal to think I am an uninvolved mom, so I will agree to chairing the school fund-raiser again this year—although it really took its toll on my family last year.
- I don't want anyone to think my spiritual walk is slipping, so I will agree to teach that Bible study class again. Although last year, my Saturday nights always seemed to be frenzied as I crammed for the next morning's lesson.

Instead of making fear-based decisions as you face opportunities, ask yourself a couple of questions:

- Does what I'm doing support my purpose?
- Does this even warrant my time and energy?

Keeping a handle on children's activities can sometimes be as hard as harnessing our own commitments. So many opportunities abound to enrich our children—sports teams, dance classes, scouting groups, and music lessons, among other things. Limiting each child to one or two organized activities per semester is usually a good rule. We can pack our children's schedules so tight they no longer have carefree hours to play.

A warm, loving, and peaceful home life (complete with family dinners together) will enrich our children more than any program we can enroll them in. That takes time at home together. They need our hugs, loving words, and attention. *Now* is the time to show our children love and teach them the lessons they will carry with them for a lifetime.

Keeping Track of Family Events

Once we have decided what activities are worthy of our time and effort, keeping track of those family events with a calendar that works well for our family is important.

What works best for you? Do you prefer a large calendar on the kitchen wall, a notebook planner, a palm-held personal digital assistant (PDA), or something else?

I have a poor memory and am a visual learner, so to stay on top of things, I have to have everything right in front of me. If I post information in a notebook in sections, I usually forget to check the sections. My solution is a one-sheet planner hand in hand with a desk calendar. On the calendar, I write down activities and details related to those activities, and on the pretty spiral notebook, I keep my working to-do list. I use one page at a time, dividing the page into broad subjects:

Things to do	Home projects (nonpressing)
Write	
	Gifts to buy
Email	
Call	Errands

By keeping everything on one page, things don't fall through the cracks as often. Throughout the day, as things come to mind, I jot them down—a name of someone I need to call, an errand I need to run. As most of the items on that page get done and marked out, I start a new page and transfer anything over that still needs to be done. I find that I usually start a new page about once a week.

If I will be running errands, I often take a more compact and portable 3-by-5-inch note card that I can carry in my pocket. If I have an especially busy day, I use the note card to write my hour-by-hour schedule and keep it in my pocket throughout the day. These ideas are simple, but they work for me.

Once a calendar system is in place, *checking* the calendar is vitally important. I once invited a friend to dinner for a Tuesday night weeks away. I put it on the calendar but failed to check the calendar as the time grew near our scheduled dinner. I also failed to mention to my husband to put the date on his calendar.

That Tuesday came. The phone rang.

"Hello?" I said.

"John and Michelle have invited us to join them for an early dinner at a local barbecue place tonight," my husband said.

Miss Spontaneity gave a quick "Yes!" and called a sitter.

After dinner, we were sitting in our family room visiting when the doorbell rang. Our invited dinner guest arrived. I could have saved both him and myself much embarrassment had I done one simple thing: checked my calendar.

Embracing Divine Interruptions

Lastly, as great as it is to have things planned out on a calendar, we must understand that God has the final word on what we do, and we must be willing to let God interrupt our plans. The Bible says, *"In his heart a man plans his course, but the* LORD *determines his steps"* (Proverbs 16:9). God appoints special missions of love for His followers. We need to recognize and embrace them. The mission may sometimes be as simple as pausing from doing the laundry to read a book to a child who asks, even if the timer is ticking (Ouch!). Or it might involve encouraging a weary cashier at the grocery store.

One hot July night after attending a gathering at a friend's house across town, I considered stopping at a corner all-night drugstore. *It's so late, but I've got to get this medication. We can hurry, and I'll get the boys to bed quickly after I get home*, I thought.

As I was putting the boys in the big metal shopping cart, a car whipped into the next parking space. A teenage girl, sobbing uncontrollably, ran over to the pay phone. *Pray with her*, I heard in my heart, but I tried to reason why I shouldn't do it: *No, it's late, and I wouldn't want to frighten her by approaching her out here in the dark parking lot. Plus, it's already past the kids' bedtimes.* And then the realization came: *Just how intimidating can a woman pushing a cart with two preschoolers be?*

So I took a deep breath, prayed for courage, and Luke 12:12 came to mind: *"The Holy Spirit will teach you at that time what you should say."*

As she slammed the phone down on the receiver and darted for her car, I asked, "Are you OK?"

"My boyfriend is a jerk!" she said.

"May I pray for you?"

She nodded her head, and tears streamed down her face.

I put my hand on her shoulder and thanked God for her and for His plans for her; then I asked Him to strengthen her, give her wisdom, and comfort her in her pain.

"Do you know Jesus as your personal Savior?" I asked.

"Yes, I do. That's why I'm so amazed you were here to pray for me," she answered with eyes full of hope and light.

I gave her a hug and watched the red taillights on her car disappear into the darkness as she drove away.

Tears filled my eyes as I drove home reflecting on God's faithfulness. "Thank You, Lord, for giving me the courage and allowing me the blessing of being Your hands and voice tonight." I added, "I also thank You for giving me the confidence that You will bring someone to be Your hands and voice for me if a time ever comes in my life when I'm hurting and all alone and need a prayer...in a place as unlikely as a dark drugstore parking lot."

During my 13 years in Phoenix, that was the only stop I ever made at that particular drugstore. God had a special ministry for me there that night, and it had much more to do with medication for the heart and soul than for the body. I pray daily that in striving to reach goals and planning, I will not miss the Holy Spirit's gentle nudge at my heart to interrupt that schedule and be a special agent of His love to someone in my path.

 ## WHAT NOW, COACH?

- What decision have you recently made that was fear based (motivated more by what you *didn't* want than by what you wanted)?
- Identify an upcoming opportunity to which you are considering committing your time. Can it pass this question emphasized four different ways, as suggested by my friend Karen Boyce, communications teacher and mother of three?
    - ❑ *Why* am I doing this now?
    - ❑ Why am *I* doing this now?
    - ❑ Why am I doing *this* now?
    - ❑ Why am I doing this *now?*
- Pray a prayer for wisdom regarding your schedule.

How Are You Running the Plays?

Just surviving the day with the many tasks and scenarios that moms deal with is a feat in and of itself. But we want to be more than survivors. To be winners, we may need to evaluate alternative means of doing a task, our attitudes, and different motivators.

Thinking through before you do is beneficial in choosing the best means available to deal with a task at hand, especially those daily home tasks that you dread. You know the ones; many times they are the ones that come each and every day. A sense of humor definitely helps. The *Baby Blues* comic strip keeps me laughing as I do my daily chores, including laundry. One strip shows Wanda putting bibs and onesies in the washing machine. She sees macaroni stuck on one bib and various vegetable stains on the others. "I'm not doing laundry—I'm making minestrone!" she says.

What is your most dreaded chore? Sometimes just putting on a pair of gloves can make a task bearable (I can touch almost anything if I have gloves on). However, one chore I deeply dread does not require gloves: emptying the dishwasher. I used to put more energy and time into dreading it than doing it! And the guilt of procrastination only compounded my negative feelings. I needed motivation and found it in my timer.

The key to getting a task done is knowing what motivates you. My timer is my motivator because I like to compete, to race the clock. I use my timer in countless other ways around my house every day. When I've been especially unmotivated about cleaning, I've had to find an even *stronger* motivator. For example, I have found that imagining company is flying in from out of town and will be arriving at my house in two hours really gets me moving! Give it some thought: What motivates you?

Before we start a job, we need to remember to think through before we do. As home managers, we need to choose and use the best means available to get a job done. The tools we use are an important part of getting the job done with a good attitude. See if you identify with me in some of the problems I have faced and the solutions I have found to help me deal with them with a better attitude:

Problem: Making sandwiches for the family. Trying to balance mayonnaise on the regular skinny butter knife and then spread with it almost drove me nuts with so many sandwiches to make.

Solution: A cake-icing spreader. I now lay out 14 pieces of bread on a large cutting board and glide the mayonnaise across the bread with wide strokes…and great joy. A user-friendly tool boosted my attitude 100 percent. Efficiency is an energy booster.

Problem: Spills on upholstered chairs. The kids often spilled their milk on our upholstered kitchen chairs.

Solution: Cover chair seat with clear vinyl. Take out screws and pop upholstered cushion off chair. Use staple gun to tightly secure clear vinyl material (available at fabric stores). This solution caused a major reduction in spill worries for me.

Problem: Bunk beds (making the top bunk). Making that top bunk bed can be especially challenging—and even more so to a mom ripe with pregnancy: Deep breathe in, stretch, pull fitted sheet corner, breathe out.

Solution: Keep a colored fitted sheet on the bed (just that). There is no need to use a top sheet, which gets tangled under the comforter anyway. In the summer, you may even take off the comforter. Dark, solid-colored fitted sheets look nice and neat. Children can grab a blanket from a bin in their closet when it's bedtime, then stuff the blanket back in there the next morning. Voilá, their bed looks neat again as the fitted sheet clings snugly to the mattress.

Think about a household chore that you dread. How much time does it realistically take? Is there a better way of doing it? Do you have a higher motive as you go about your tasks? Here's to efficiently and lovingly doing the laundry…and making minestrone!

 WHAT NOW, COACH?
- What dreaded chores could you delegate?
- List three motivating factors to help you deal with your most dreaded chore.

Naptime Is Prime Time

When you have a baby or preschooler in the family, maximizing naptime daily is key to getting things done in the home that need to be done. A routine nap schedule benefits both the baby and family. Not only does the baby know what to anticipate, so does the mom. Young babies typically need three one- to two-hour naps each day. At about six months, they can usually drop to one morning and one afternoon nap. And one two- to three-hour nap per day will usually do for children 15 months and older.

Let's look at some naptime strategies that will help you make the most of that prime time.

Honor the Naptime Rule
And what is the naptime rule? **Do only what you *cannot* do when the baby is awake.** Tackling projects at home with babies and preschoolers takes *strategy*. You must make the most of

those few minutes or hours that you are not having to give 100 percent attention to them. Think through before you do. Do during baby's naptimes whatever you *cannot* do when baby is awake. These tasks are often things that require concentration or involve hazards.

Examples of Tasks to Do During Baby's Naptime
- Make important phone calls.
- Study the Bible.
- Pay bills.
- Iron clothes.
- Balance the checkbook.
- Write correspondence.
- Get dinner started to help that hectic dinner prep time go a little smoother.
- Nap.

Note: If *you* are in need of a nap, that becomes top priority during baby's nap.

And what things do you *not* want to waste prime time doing during their naptime? Things that require minimal concentration—things you can do while interacting with your children.

Examples of Tasks to Do During Baby's Awake Time
- Bring the house into order.
- Pull weeds in the garden.
- Water plants.
- Cut coupons.
- Fold laundry.
- Clean the kitchen.

One exception to these suggestions is when you've been out all morning and have come into a house of unmade beds, dirty kitchen, and other messes. If you have just put the baby down and know you have some things you *must* tend to during naptime, allow yourself 12 to 15 minutes on the timer to bring the house to some semblance of order. (It's amazing how much can be done in that amount of time.) When that has been done, you may forge ahead with the things that must be done without feeling your house is out of control. Sometimes it's hard to stop when that timer rings, but try to hold yourself to it and move to an important task during your prime work time—baby's naptime.

Working moms need to be all the more masterful at this, as they have so much to accomplish during their days off. Think through before you do.

Maximize Naptime

I don't know of many things more discouraging to a mother than babies who are awakened early from their naps. Maximizing naptime adds hours to a mom's day, and she also has a more rested baby. Here are a few tips for helping your child get a good nap.

Minimize sound and light interruptions. Naptime sound buffers (such as fans, humidifiers, sound machines, and radios) muffle the sounds of household noises (such as older siblings) that might wake the babies prematurely. Also, shades on the windows are helpful to darken nurseries that have an afternoon western exposure.

Speaking of getting awakened during naptime, on Sunday afternoons (or daily if a newborn is in the house), I often try to sneak in an afternoon nap. To discourage the older boys from waking me from my nap, I let them know that if they wake Mom from a nap to ask a question, the answer will always be an automatic *no*.

Aim for full naps. I found that my children often stirred and cried out about 45 minutes into their nap. Knowing they needed to get at least one and a half hours for an optimum nap, I set the timer for 5 minutes to see if they would settle back down into their deeper sleep, and most of the time after less than 5 minutes, they continued their nap. When they woke up happy and cooing instead of crying out, I knew that they had gotten their full nap.

Be creative. If two of your children who share a room both need a nap, you may need to think creatively. Putting two children in the same room to nap is not a combination for success. It is helpful to move one child to the master bedroom. If the weather permits, make one child a pallet up in the play set for naptime. Who wouldn't love a nap that ends with a ride down the slide with a favorite teddy bear?

 ## WHAT NOW, COACH?

- Are you wasting prime time by doing things during baby's naptime that don't require concentration or focus—things that can be done when baby is awake? List those things.
- List three things that you can do *only* when baby is asleep.

APPLICATION

12

Party Solutions

Preschool birthday parties can get so out of hand. Marketers want you to believe that you need to buy all the party paraphernalia available in the stores in order to have a special party. I've seen many stressed-out, overworked, and broke parents attempting to provide their child with what they think is the most special birthday party ever, but often they are so involved in the elaborate production that all the parents' attention goes to the party instead of to the child.

Creative and Economical Parties

Children's parties don't have to be expensive or elaborate to be special. Think creatively! Plato's saying, "Necessity is the mother of invention," has been true for me with birthday parties. I've taken a look around my house and have come up with simple themes from things we already had on hand. By doing this, I've managed to do 21 out of 22 kid parties for under $20—including cake, decorations, drinks, treat bags, and a craft!

Hints for a Preschooler's Party

- Include one inexpensive craft, face-painting related to the theme (a one-time investment), theme-related version of the pin the tail on the donkey game (drawn on poster board), and a relay game.
- Decorate with theme-related toys or figurines you have on hand.
- Make treat bags out of lunch sacks decorated with stickers or drawings.
- Consider a less expensive and often more popular alternative to birthday cake:
  - ❑ Cupcakes
  - ❑ Cake baked in ice-cream cones and topped off with icing
  - ❑ Rice Krispies treat "cupcakes" (Kids don't do the typical lick-off-the-icing trick—they eat every bite! Make a regular batch of Rice Krispies treats, and press into the bottom half of greased muffin tins. Then make another batch, adding food coloring, and mound on top to look like iced muffins. You could even add sprinkles before they cool.)
  - ❑ Large birthday cookie (Use premade chocolate chip cookie dough to make the large cookie. Write *Happy Birthday* on it with icing, and add a few theme-related items to top it off.
- Invite only as many children as the child is in years. (This is a lesson that most first-time parents end up learning the hard way!)
- For a two-year-old's birthday, open gifts after the guests leave. (I've witnessed many a tearful misunderstanding in two-year-old guests.)

Theme Ideas for a Young Child's Party

- **Cowboys/Indians:** Put bandanas on the cowboys and paint mustaches on their faces with face paint; let Indians make beaded headbands and apply face paint for their war paint.
- **Ladybugs:** Use red cups with black dots drawn on them; sculpt with red and black play dough; using face paint, draw ladybugs on guests' cheeks.
- **Dinosaurs:** Have a "dino dig" in the sandbox in search of dinosaur gummies in zipper-sealed clear snack bags; use on-hand toys as cake decorations.
- **Clowns:** Temporarily inflate balloons, and write out invitations with a permanent marker on them; then deflate and send in envelopes filled with confetti. Paint clown faces on guests, and let them dress up in oversize shorts and shirts, suspenders, bow ties, or whatever you have on hand. Serve popcorn and peanuts.
- **Farm:** Play pin the tail on the donkey and duck, duck, goose; use toy farm animals on the cake. Have a hayride by pulling kids around the yard in a hay-filled wagon.
- **Sports party:** Dress in uniforms; play relay games with balls; give each a whistle; parent wears a referee shirt; draw balls on cheeks with face paint; have a cheerleader serve popcorn in megaphones; decorate pennants.
- **Pirates:** Draw eye patches with face paint on the children, and tie bandanas on their heads; use a treasure map to hunt for treat bags; make swords out of large cardboard pieces and spyglasses out of toilet paper tubes and cellophane.
- **Breakfast party:** Decorate pancakes; dress in pj's, decorate a pillowcase or a place mat.
- **Costume party:** Give homemade ribbon awards for *each* costume—Most Creative, Funniest, Scariest, etc. (The kids will *love* this.)

- **Pink party:** Participants wear pink, eat and drink pink, and bring pink. (My friend Karianne Wood came up with this fun idea.)
- **Dogs:** Eat hot dogs out of dog dishes; make headbands with floppy ears; create with face paint a dog face on each child; play pin the bone on the dog's mouth.

The theme possibilities are endless. Come up with themes that reflect the interests of *your* children. Remember, the point is to honor the birthday child and make him or her feel special. A few creative simple touches can make a day delightful.

Family Birthday Traditions

Build in your own fun family traditions. We have a hat we call the "birthday hat" that the honored guest wears at a family meal on his or her birthday. I like to present a pint of birthday cake–flavored ice cream to the honoree at breakfast and tell that child the ice cream can be eaten anytime that day (yes, even at breakfast [Eeek!]), and that it will be in the freezer for him or her to freely partake of throughout the day.

As we've added more members to our family, we've also realized that alternating birthday party years greatly simplifies our life. Each child gets a party every other year. The "off" year, we do something fun as a family and allow the birthday child to have a friend over for a special get-together or fun outing.

 WHAT NOW, COACH?

- Considering your children's special interests, list two possible party themes for each child.
- Think of three activities that would be fun family traditions to establish for birthday celebrations.

APPLICATION

13

Pacing the Marathon Mom

Let us run with perseverance the race marked out for us.
—Hebrews 12:1

Part of thinking through before you do is making sure you pace yourself by building in energizing activities to help you through the marathon of being a mom. We moms need to take care of ourselves physically and emotionally so we will have the energy to take care of all those who are dependent on us. Rest and rewards along the way enable us to persevere; they turn our marathon into manageable sprints.

Get Your Rest

Rest, although hard to come by for a mother of little ones, is easy to define. It's stopping, sitting down, and propping the feet up for a 15-minute break to read a good book; it's taking a bubble bath or lying down for a nap during the baby's naptime (the latter tops the charts for mothers of newborns).

Reward and Refresh Yourself

Rewards can be any number of things, depending on your preferences and personality. What do you find to be enriching and enlivening? Singing, playing the piano, painting, reading, or gardening? If you can't think of what that might be, reflect back on your childhood and youth: What activities brought you the most satisfaction and joy? Many of our creative loves seem to get pushed to the side (or even allowed to die) when children come along. It's important to continue to nurture that creative part of yourself, even if only in tiny ways.

Reaching out to those who are in need can also be an energy booster. In ministering to others by a kind card or gesture, our spirits, too, are nurtured. The Bible tells us, *"It is more blessed to give than to receive"* (Acts 20:35). Outreach activity also reminds us that there is a bigger picture out there beyond our world of diapers and laundry.

By the way, sitting in front of the television rarely counts as an energy refresher. So turn off the tube.

Frequently Foster Friendships

We were made with the need to connect with others. But according to women's ministry leader Beverly White Hislop, women today are facing increased isolation and disconnection from other women:

> A woman's sense of self, of who she is, is organized around being able to make and maintain relationships.... The impact of this threat of disrupting connection is perceived not as just a loss of relationships but as something closer to a total loss of self.* Maintaining connections with others can be life giving to women, while loss can be life threatening.
>
> Today, women have to be intentional about finding ways to enter community, to connect with one another. The need for input, care, and shepherding from other women is heightened even further because these kinds of relationships are not readily available. They are not built into the everyday life of most women.
> —Beverly White Hislop, *Shepherding a Woman's Heart*, with reference at asterisk (*) to Jean Baker Miller, *Toward a New Psychology of Women* (Boston: Beacon, 1976)

Let's look at the ways a few energized mom superheroes connect with other women.

Scrapbook Sally: She is my shutterbug friend. She makes a point to get together with a few friends the first Friday evening of every month to work on preserving family memories through scrapbooking. She shares her latest frustrations, laughs until she cries, snacks on trail mix, and feels good that she is not only catching up with friends but also completing a few more pages in her family album.

Bible Study Billie: She is single, working full-time, and worn out most of the time. But Billie found a nearby church that offers a women's Bible study on Wednesday nights. Her children are well cared for (and learn a few things about the Bible themselves), she makes some deep friendships in her small group, and she is encouraged, making it easier for her to get through two more workdays before the weekend.

Cheesecake Factory Chelsea: She is home full-time with a four-month-old, a two-year-old, and a four-year-old. Her husband spends many hours working and commuting, and she is lonely. Out of desperation one day, she called the teenager down the street to babysit, so she could meet a friend for lunch. Seeing what a difference a couple of hours out of the house made, she now schedules lunch with friends every other week on Tuesdays. Her sitter has even agreed to stay a couple of extra hours, so she can do her grocery shopping too. Her husband comments that he sees a spark in her again.

Game-Night Glenda: She keeps her preschoolers during the day and attempts to help cover the bills by running an eBay business in the evenings. She feels the weight of the stress of meeting the needs of their kids and home, while making sure she is diligent in her business. Thankfully, Glenda has a neighbor who invited her to a monthly Bunco night with a dozen other women. At first, Glenda didn't think she could fit one more thing into her busy schedule, but she realized that this fun game night (which is more about socializing than it is strategy) is like a lifeline to her during this intense season of working for her family and her business.

MOPS Member Molly: Her husband was recently transferred. She not only moved away from her parents for the first time, but she also has just become a mom. She had many questions and was seeking some help on the Internet when she came across the

MOPS (Mothers of Preschoolers) International Web site. She saw that a MOPS group was meeting at a church only a mile from her house and decided to give it a try. She is getting answers to her questions, having opportunity to vent her frustrations to women who understand, and gaining encouraging friendships.

YMCA Juanita: Having recently joined a YMCA near her home, she is feeling great about getting back into shape. Her kids, ages 18 months and three years, enjoy the kids club. She participates in the early aerobics class and has made new friends there. She also is reading at least two books a month while riding the stationary bike (uninterrupted reading time); she's enjoying the great plots and has decided to give up daytime soaps altogether. After this workout time to herself, she feels renewed to go home and spend time reading to her kids.

Even on very busy days, I try to take at least 15 minutes to sit down and read a book or take a few minutes to chat outside with a neighbor. Do you feel you just don't have the time? Remember, the greater the challenge, the more diligent you, as a mom, must be to make sure you are building energy-renewers into your schedule.

 ## WHAT NOW, COACH?

- What enriching and enlivening activity can you add to your daily schedule? ...weekly schedule? ...bimonthly or monthly schedule?
- Get your calendar (yes, now), and record the days you will add these activities.

APPLICATION
14

Mom, Masterful Milestone Marker

> *The faintest ink is more powerful*
> *than the strongest memory.*
> —Old Chinese proverb

Recording Children's Milestones

The last part of thinking through before you do involves having a long-range outlook. Is it important to you to remember milestones in your children's growth? Then start a journal, or if you are more comfortable using the computer, keep your records on disk. I have a clothbound journal for each of my children; in these journals, I record cute sayings, firsts, thoughts, and prayers.

If you think your writing has to be perfect when journaling, you will be too intimidated to start a journal. I gave my dear grandmother a journal to record stories from her childhood. She wrote her thoughts on small pieces of scratch paper, with plans to transfer it, perfectly written, at a later date. A few years later, she passed on to be with the Lord. It would mean so much to me to have her handwritten stories in the journal that now sits empty on the shelf.

When I start to get paralyzed with that perfectionist thinking, I have to ask myself, "What is my goal?" My goal, as it turns out, is to have *something* to look back on and pass on to my children some day. So I just do it. It doesn't have to be elaborate. Some days, it may be just a date and a quick note to jog a memory. Other days, I might take more time and write out a heartfelt prayer for the character God is building in them, my hopes for them, and His plans for them. I've tried to jot down their favorites every year too (favorite food, favorite song, favorite book, best friend, and such). Interviews are also fun to document: What are their dreams for the future? What do they most enjoy right now? Those things are fun to look back on as their interests change.

Recording Personal Spiritual Growth Milestones

And what about milestones in your spiritual growth? Do you want a record to look back on so you can see the prayers that have been answered? Is God working in your life in visible ways? Don't let your days slip to weeks and weeks to years without recording God's activity in your life. Simple, quick notes and dates can turn into such treasures as you look back on them in years to come.

When my first son was a baby, I realized the importance of recording answers to prayer. This realization came when we were in the mountains in Flagstaff, Arizona, at a Fellowship of Christian Athletes camp. While Dillon was napping, I was lying on the bed in the quiet dorm room, reading a passage from the Bible. As I read, the words seemed to pop off the page at me. Those words gave me the answer to something I'd been asking of the Lord. I sat there for some time, overjoyed, pondering it. Then this thought came to my mind (which I believe was from the Lord): *The Creator of the universe has just spoken to you. Do you think it is worth your time to write it down?* I quickly fumbled for a notebook and wrote down what He had said.

Since that time, I've tried to write down everything I feel God is telling me, so that I can reflect on it more and not forget the ways I've been directed to go. I've been blessed many times as I've looked in my spiritual journal and seen the significance in the dates and things into which God has led me.

My fourth pregnancy was quite a spiritual journey. The summer before I got pregnant, my heart had been burdened like never before with the importance of prayer. I sat in my living room and wrote in my journal early one morning in June: "New resolve and commitment for earlier hours, more solitude with God." I had a continuous passion as never before to be in prayer and reading God's Word morning, noon, and night with whatever minutes I could find.

As I spent time in the Bible and in prayer, I felt the Lord was telling me that we, as a church, had to have great faith like that of the Israeli priests who stepped into the roaring Jordan River at flood level while carrying the ark of the covenant, their most prized possession (Joshua 3).

Every step of my pregnancy, I felt God showing me how that step related to what He was birthing spiritually at our church, and I recorded it. And it seemed that everywhere I went, I heard Steven Curtis Chapman's song, "Great Expectations," so it was recorded many times in my journal. I kept saying, "I've never been so expectant in all my life" (both physically and spiritually).

A fund-raising campaign was just beginning to kick off at our church; it was going to require a major financial sacrifice for many of us. Chris and I felt, after much prayer, that the Lord had led us to commit to giving nearly half of our yearly income for three years, and we knew many others were called to a similar commitment—a commitment beyond anything that would work on paper.

As I pondered my early July due date, I saw in the church bulletin one Sunday that the first day of sacrificial giving, which would indeed require great faith, was to be June 25, 2000. I wondered deep down if that could possibly be my son's due date. Later that week, I was reading over past journal entries and found where I had written one common Saturday summer morning, "New resolve and commitment for earlier hours, more solitude with God 6/25/99." I realized that exactly one year before the day requiring great faith, the Lord had begun preparing me through prayer. Right then, I knew in my heart we would not be waiting until July to have our son. I ran to tell my husband to expect our son on June 25. *Sure, honey*, he probably thought.

My water broke on June 24. As we backed the car out of the driveway to go to the hospital, the song "Great Expectations" came on the radio and stayed on the entire time until we pulled into the hospital parking lot!

Micah Bradford (meaning "broad river crosser who is like the Lord") was born the eve of June 25, 2000. And Sunday morning,

I woke up to three immediate opportunities (one after the other) to share very directly God's love and grace with three people: my tending nurse, pediatrician, and obstetrician. It was June 25, 2000, and joy poured out of my heart in thankfulness for what God was doing.

Three years later, in the worship service celebrating the third anniversary of our campaign called Beyond Belief, our worship leader, Robert Comeaux, sang a song. And what song do you suppose he sang? You are right—"Great Expectations." Tears streamed down my cheeks as I was reminded of God's great love, sovereignty, and faithfulness...as whispered to me from the pages of my own journal.

 ## WHAT NOW, COACH?

- Write a plan of action for recording milestones in your children's growth.
- Decide on a plan for recording milestones in your spiritual growth.
- Get started today, even if taking only a small step.

REMOVE AND APPROVE

Our homes and lives are stuffed with so many unnecessary things, which slow us down and complicate our lives—taking up our time and giving us more to do. But you can learn to remove and approve. Eliminate the unnecessary things in your life, and see what a difference it makes.

APPLICATION

15

Clutter Busting

Ridding your home of clutter is one of the *most important* things you can do to have an orderly and efficient home, and it is probably the *most difficult* to do. Then once it is done, the clutter beast still must be tamed daily.

If you are preparing to sell your house, you are, no doubt, taming the beast. You must. What about the rest of us? Let's consider making the "house ready for show" condition the norm for our homes. Looking at our homes through the eyes of prospective buyers will give us fresh ideas on changes we can make to bring order.

Decluttering can seem so overwhelming that many people avoid it altogether. The key is to tackle one small portion at a time, focusing on two areas: the seen and the unseen.

Rid your home of visible clutter one room at a time. Take an honest look at each room. Taking pictures of each wall will help you assess your room and also show you how far you've come once you are done. Do you have wall-to-wall furniture and stuff, or do you have breaks along the walls for the eye to rest? Evaluate one wall at a time, removing unnecessary items.

After bringing your house to order by eliminating visible clutter room by room, you may then move to the next step.

Remove unseen clutter—that unnecessary stuff lurking in drawers, closets, and cabinets. Divide the job into small parts in order to see that your goal is attainable. Work closet by closet, room by room. One day you might declutter three out of nine drawers in a dresser and the next day maybe only one—but the point to remember is that you are making progress.

You won't believe how quickly you can win the war on clutter if you are diligent to make a schedule and stick with it every day for a few weeks.

Get-It-Done Idea

Start a decluttering notebook:

- Get a notebook, and divide it into two sections: "Visible Clutter" and "Unseen Clutter" (drawers, closets, cabinets).
- Walk throughout the house and write down areas that need to be addressed, breaking each room down into small parts.
- Leave space to record your target date, date you actually worked on it, and time spent. This will track your work.
- Plan some incentives/rewards along the way, and record them in your notebook. Going out to lunch with a friend or buying those shoes you've been wanting might help motivate you, though your greatest reward will be the joy of clutter-free spaces.

- Get to work. If you clean out two drawers every day for two weeks, you will organize 28 drawers. Or set the timer for 15 or 20 minutes each day, and do whatever you can do within that time. You might be surprised.

Steps to Decluttering

Decluttering requires mental and physical activity:
- Determine the function of the area you are addressing.
- Empty the contents of the area onto a sheet (dump the drawer).
- Put back only what is needed in that area.

This will leave you with a clutter-free space. It will also leave you with a mound of things. These leftover items will go in one of three places:
- A **big** throwaway can (No one can use the item.)
- A giveaway box (You no longer have need for the item, but someone else might.)
- A put-away bin (You still need or could use the item, but it belongs somewhere else.)

Processing the Pain of Purging Personal Possessions

Parting with things is the most emotional aspect of organizing a home. Sentimental attachments and what-if-I-need-it fears make us clench our fists and hold tightly to things. But the larger the item, the more you'll have to weigh whether it's worth keeping. Every item you choose to keep costs you space and time.

To make it easier, pray a prayer for wisdom and courage, then use self-talk. Decide which of the following questions is most motivating to you, then ask yourself that question over and over and over again:
- Who could be getting good use out of this item?
- Is this item worth the time and space it takes to keep it?
- It's a special dress, but will I really ever wear it again? Do I have a picture of myself in it?
- What is the worst thing that could happen if I got rid of this?

Find a New Use for Items

If you are no longer using a furniture piece or another special item, yet you just can't seem to part with it, consider a different use for it. Five years ago, my friend Kristi moved into a new home. The high ceilings and vast entryway dwarfed one of her favorite pieces, a beautiful antique buffet. After investing in a larger buffet, she put the original one in the attic. Last week she was organizing a large closet near her entryway and needed a holder for gift-wrapping supplies. She didn't buy something new. She simply went up to her attic, dusted off the buffet, and carried it down to serve as "Gift Wrapping Central." Kristi feels joy each time she opens the closet door—and her attic is clearer.

This kind of creative thinking takes effort. We grow accustomed to where we keep pieces and how we use them. When I have something I'm struggling to part with, I try to take a step back and pretend that I'm seeing it for the first time at a sale and it is marked at a giveaway price. I ask myself, "How could I use this piece in my house?" That's when I start thinking creatively: *Could I paint it? Could I use it in a nontraditional way?*

But What if I Need It?

A couple of years ago, my husband and I started the New Year with a big cleaning binge. Our fourth son was 18 months old, and we finally got rid of all the baby things that had been cluttering our attic for eight years.

We felt relieved to be completely past the baby stage and all the stuff that it entails. We smiled and patted each other on the back as we admired our clear and organized attic.

I also gave away my maternity clothes, clearing a large space in my closet. Before doing that, I asked myself, "What is the worst thing that could happen if I got rid of this?" I answered, "Get pregnant."

Just a few weeks later, my husband and I stared in disbelief at two stripes on a little white wand. The "worst thing" *had* happened. I still couldn't help but be delighted with my organized, spacious closet.

A couple of friends offered to let me borrow their maternity clothes—more stylish than mine—and I made a small investment in a few basic pieces. I realized I didn't need much to get me through those months.

We borrowed a baby swing, baby tub, car seat, and other items from friends, which we promptly passed back when our fifth child, daughter Karis, no longer needed them.

Are you overwhelmed with all the clutter in your home? Let it go. Make a plan and get started. Skipping over the application part of this chapter will cost you much. Freedom comes when you realize you can do without the things you thought you had to have.

WHAT NOW, COACH?

- Begin your war on clutter. For review, here again are the steps to removing clutter:
  - ✓ Determine the function of the area being decluttered.
  - ✓ *Empty* the area.
  - ✓ Put back only what is needed in that area.
  - ✓ Put leftover items into one of three containers—the throwaway, put-away, or giveaway bin.
- Choose one area of a room, and work 15 minutes to remove visible clutter. List area, function of area, and how the 15 minutes went. Are you surprised at what you accomplished in 15 minutes?
- Choose one area of *unseen* clutter (closet, drawer, or cabinet), and work 15 minutes to remove the clutter. List area, function of area, and how the 15 minutes went. Are you surprised at what you accomplished in 15 minutes?

16

Reflections on a Kitchen Sink

Family life revolves around the kitchen sink—period. Keeping a clear and clean sink during extra-busy times when the house looks like it has been turned upside down will preserve our sanity. When my sink is clear, my mind seems to be clearer too. It's a simple strategy, but delivers a punch. Sink clutter can take us down faster than regular household clutter—it can threaten to take us all down, depending on the magnitude of the stack. When it comes to sink clutter, remove and approve.

- To stay on schedule, run the dishwasher every day, even if it is only half full.
- Empty dishwasher as soon as possible.
- Rinse dirty dishes and load them into washer immediately. (Doesn't that sound so much simpler than it is?)

Keeping the kitchen sink clear will also give you the confidence and strength to tackle the mess in other rooms. Try keeping your kitchen sink clean and clear for an entire week, and see if you don't notice a difference in your quality of life.

It took me years to realize how the discipline of keeping a clear and clean kitchen sink could bless my life. I once joked with my husband, offering a slight revision of Philippians 4:13 (NKJV): *"'I can do all things through Christ who strengthens me'*...if my kitchen sink is clean." Amen.

 ## WHAT NOW, COACH?

- Assignment: Throughout every day this week, be diligent to keep your kitchen sink clear and clean.
- After the week, ask yourself, "Did the clean sink affect my attitude?"

Papers, Papers, Everywhere

Households received 74.2 billion pieces of mail in the US Postal Service's 2003 fiscal year, according to the agency's annual Household Diary Study. Two out of five households received at least 30 or more mail pieces weekly in 2003, making the yearly mail pieces those homes received total more than 1,560. The USPS is only one source bringing papers to us daily. And what do we do with those papers? First, we stack them on tables, counters, and any other raised, flat surface. Then we begin the floor stacks. And before long, each room is a sea of stacks.

Daily we must apply the remove and approve strategy in order to keep papers under control.

Discard unneeded mail immediately. Take an objective look at the mail and decide whether it really needs to be saved. The bulk of it can usually go straight to the recycle trash bin.

Transfer important information to the calendar. Immediately discard informational papers after posting the information provided.

Discard most of your children's work sheets and artwork (Ouch!). Save only the very best pieces of your children's artwork—the ones that show their development and talent or have special meanings attached. Record the child's name and age on the keepers, then put them in a place designated for saving their best artwork; this can be a file, drawer, or bin.

Capture the memory of a child's artwork in a photograph. Large papers offer great breadth for expressive young artists, but they don't fit neatly into files. One option is to take a photograph of the child holding the artwork, and then discard the piece. In Derek's scrapbook, I was able to display 16 pieces of his oversize artwork on one 12-by-12-inch page. One photograph is of Derek holding two of his paintings. The other pictures are of his artwork only—two pieces in each photograph. I think we look at his art more often now than if I had saved it in a large art portfolio, which would be stored in the back of a dark closet.

If you must save a piece of artwork that is an awkward size, just fold it in half and place it in the "save" drawer. Another option is to display the artwork on the garage walls (*after* first discussing the idea with your husband, of course, if this is his domain). The art will put a smile on your face each time you pull your car into the garage.

Discard or pass on magazines, keeping only the best articles. Tear out only the A+ articles you must have, file them in idea files under specific subject headings, such as birthday parties, remodeling projects, organization, and scrapbook pages. (We'll talk more about files in the next chapter.) Because ideas on every subject imaginable are available on the Internet, we have the freedom to say no to saving everything in home files—we are free to say no to stacks and stacks of magazines in our home saved just in case we need *something* from them *some time* in the future.

Create a place for pending papers. In order to avoid piles of "keepers for now" on your countertop, create a pending file (can be a drawer or folder). This file is for things like book order forms from school, fund-raising forms and information, Bible verse memorization sheets, and party invitations with directions. Keep this file near the kitchen to hold papers that require action before discarding.

When dealing with papers, remember to remove, then step back and take a look—you will approve. Now go fill some trash cans!

 ## WHAT NOW, COACH?

- Today, set the timer for ten minutes. Fill one grocery bag with unnecessary papers (extra magazines, papers piled on the counter, and such), and throw them in the recycle trash bin.
- Create an idea file.
- Establish a place for pending papers.

APPLICATION 18

Bye-Bye Toys, Hello Joys

Do you ever suspect Buzz Lightyear and his comrades are plotting to overtake your home? When was the last time you were booby-trapped by one of the little army men, who launched you three feet into the air with a scream when you stepped on him in the dark? When was the last time you felt demoralized by Slinky toys, Little Bo Peeps, and Barbie doll accessories lying all over your child's bedroom floor? I'm not making this up—toys can get to you if you let them outnumber you by too great a ratio.

Steps to Toy Joy

The following ideas will help you make peace with the toys.

Use shelves, not a toy box. Large toy boxes often end up getting stuffed until they are filled to the brim, making an organization system impossible. Shelves allow the children to see everything, and easily remove and replace toys one at a time.

Rotate toys. Pack a large container with toys, and put it away for a few months. Your children will enjoy their current toys more, having fewer options. And when you bring the container out in a couple of months and unload it, you will think it is Christmas, as your kids squeal in delight. Then pack up the toys that have been available for play the last few months, and put those away for a while.

Carefully consider purchases at birthdays and Christmas. Avoid large toys as much as possible. They cost more than big bucks—they cost space. Battery-powered toys continue to cost you money. Give and encourage grandparents to give mostly expendable items, such as food or entertainment gift cards.

Another expendable gift you can give is your own gift certificate, giving the children a special day with Dad or Mom doing some activity the children love to do.

Keep only the best toys to pass down to younger siblings.
Remove all other toys. Toys must be culled on a regular basis
or stuff can get overwhelming. If you have only one child, this
may not seem too large a task. But the more children you add to
the family, the greater the challenge is. When Christmas comes
to the Stull family, if every child receives six toys (which is not
uncommon, when you consider two sets of grandparents, friends,
family, and Santa), then 30 new toys enter our house. The added
challenge is that I hold on to toys for ages spanning eight years.
The thing I must constantly tell myself is to hold on to staple
toys only.

One example of a staple toy is **stacking cups.** Just think about
the value and versatility of stacking cups:
- Provide a variety of stacking options
- Teach spatial skills, colors, and sometimes numbers
  and animals
- Can be used with play dough
- Don't require batteries
- Make great bath toys
- Hold Cheerios at snacktime
- Are small, inexpensive, and portable (though I choose
  not to let them out of my house)
- Fit inside each other for efficient use of space
- Entertain kids of all ages

(Doesn't that make you want to run out and buy a set of
stacking cups right now?)

Keep only toys that meet at least three of the following criteria:
- Is it fun for your child?
- Does your child actually play with it?
- Does it teach new skills or imaginative play?
- Is it easy to store?
- Has it stood the test of time?

If it doesn't need batteries, that's all the better. Regularly eliminate
all others. So what do you do with the extras? Donate toys to

a teacher's classroom reward box, or give them to a friend who has just had her first baby. You might even sell a few of the more valuable items through eBay.

Space for Imagination

Clearing some space on toy shelves also allows our children the opportunity to create their own toys once in a while. (Three cheers for growing imaginations!) With a little free time, children can use their creativity to come up with hours of fun: paper airplanes, paper tops, plastic jug rhythm instruments, and sandwich "swords" (made by the boy whose mom said, "I will *never* promote violence by giving my son a toy sword").

Our friends the Crouches introduced our children to silly balloon games. They lived in a small house and were good at keeping toys pared to a minimum. Balloons provided them hours of fun and inexpensive enjoyment.

Chris orchestrates paper airplane contests from the second-story landing that overlooks our family room. He sets buckets and pans down below and offers rewards for hitting specific targets. One night Dillon's plane took a nosedive into the opening of a skillet's handle to win the grand prize—a triple-scoop ice-cream sundae. Bye-bye toys, hello joys!

 WHAT NOW, COACH?

- Set the timer for 15 minutes. In that time, fill at least one bag full of outgrown or extra toys to donate or pass on. As a learning activity, involve your children (if you dare!).
- Fill one bin with toys to rotate, and store it away for a while.

19

Ring, Ring, Ring

Phone interruptions. These two words together make for a good laugh as I reflect on one trying day in the summer of 2002. I was seven months pregnant, had just moved our family of six and all our possessions one week before, and was attempting to unpack boxes when the doorbell rang.

"A package for me?!" my two-year-old exclaimed.

Micah pulled a brightly colored battery-powered Talking Toucan out of the box. "What is it?"

"What is it?"

"It talks!"

"It talks!"

"Cool!"

"Cool!" The toucan repeated every word said.

Meanwhile, my phone was ringing off the hook. I was fielding calls from parents of my 40 art students; they were calling about classes that were due to start in two weeks.

"Yes, he'll need a 9-by-12-inch drawing pad."

"Yes, he'll need a 9-by-12-inch drawing pad," the toucan piped.

Then came a call from a retreat director who had questions regarding my planned topics for each session. As I was trying to answer calmly and professionally—"I will send the original handout to you by mail next week, and I'm prayerfully considering..."—I heard, Mr. Toucan repeat, "I will send the original handout to you by mail next week, and I'm prayerfully considering...."

Trying to get away from that stuffed copycat bird, I went from room to room while conversing with this retreat director—but to no avail; the four boys followed me wherever I went, laughing hilariously because the toucan repeated my every word. I kept trying to escape without locking doors (lest the followers begin to cry out loudly) and without tripping over boxes I couldn't see because of my protruding tummy. All the while, I was trying to stay focused with my thoughts and poised and professional in my speech so as not to worry this retreat director, who had not met me, her speaker, in person yet. Can you picture it!

We must remember as moms that the phone is a tool to help us, not something to make our life more complicated and hectic. These days, people expect instant communication with us at all times. This can be a good thing, but often calls are just an interruption or come at inconvenient times.

Manage the Phone—Don't Let It Manage You

Take steps to remove phone distractions, and learn to manage the phone rather than letting it dictate your day.

Let your phone take messages. These days we have many tools available to keep us from missing important calls. If I am helping or teaching the children or working on a project, I often let the answering machine take messages. Later, at my convenience, I return the calls all at once. Caller ID helps me catch pressing calls.

Evaluate your phone habits by logging calls. Consider a weeklong logging of your phone calls. If you are home during the day, you might be amazed at how much time you spend on the phone. Find a way to set some parameters for yourself. My friend and I found that we were spending too much time talking on the phone, so we decided to correspond more by email.

Beware of babbling. Although it is important to keep friendship connections, the habit of nonstop chatting with friends on the phone is not good for you or your little ones. And it is even worse for your marriage. Keeping phone conversations short when your husband is home and giving him attention help in meeting one of his greatest needs—the need for respect.

Be safe when driving and talking on your cell phone. Using a hands-free phone system in the car will allow you to keep both hands on the steering wheel. But we must remember that as our children get older, car time is one of the last places we have them as our captive audience. I'm not against cars wired up with movies, especially during long trips. A portable television and DVDs have magically shaved hours off of our cross-country trips. But a never-ending movie loop combined with a preoccupied mom with a phone to her ear does nothing to build mother-child intimacy. We need to get off our phones and do some fun kid quizzes to stay connected with our children. "What's your favorite color and why?" "What makes you happiest?" "What was the best thing that happened to you today?" Connect and reconnect.

If you work from home, minimize phone distractions. Think creatively to make the most of the time you spend with your children when they are awake and still get your work done. Determine the best time for you to make or receive phone calls—perhaps during baby's independent playtime, during a favorite educational television show or video, or during naptime. Then let associates and clients know the best hours to reach you, and take care of the bulk of your phone calls during those hours.

Working from your home is a wonderful privilege as well as a challenge. You must be strategic to successfully and simultaneously work from home and mother preschoolers. Work as hard for kid connections as you do for client connections.

According to family expert Tim Kimmel, "We [the professional world] collectively spend billions on ads, psychological profiles, and demographic studies so that we may woo, wow, and win our clients. Meanwhile, back at the condominium [or our home], a few extremely impressionable souls just wait to be programmed" (*Raising Kids Who Turn Out Right*). We often overlook the incredible influence we have in our homes—influence freely given to us by God.

Maybe you're not running from kids and toucans, but has your phone become a wall blocking communication between you and your family? Find ways to minimize phone interruptions and interact more meaningfully with your children and husband. They need you...today.

 **WHAT NOW, COACH?**

- List one change you are making this week to keep your phone from controlling your time.
- Identify the best time blocks for you to handle your necessary calls.

APPLICATION

Distancing Distractions

As we consider the things that we must remove from our homes and lives in order to have a peaceful, joyful, efficient home life, we must also consider removing from our hearts and minds the things that hinder a peaceful, joyful heart.

One of my favorite verses to pray to the Lord is, *"May every fiber of my being unite in reverence to your name"* (Psalm 86:11 TLB). You may be thinking, *That sounds great, but how can I realistically do that considering today's society?*

It takes effort—but can be done.

Minimize the Message of the Culture

If we are followers of Christ, we are living counter to most of what our culture tells us every day. But there *are* steps we can take to minimize the message of the culture and maximize the message of God's truth in our lives.

Turn off the television. Every hour of every day, television offers us hundreds of programs, most of little or no value. If time is money, why are we choosing to spend it on something that doesn't move us closer to any of our goals?

During the day, we watch only a few children's educational programs. CDs playing praise music and other songs fill our hearts and minds with reminders of the truths of Christ. Evenings we must stay on a strict schedule of getting homework finished, practices done, dinner, and baths. After the children are in bed, my husband and I often select a program to watch (usually as we fold the daily two to three loads of laundry), but we are not enslaved to the television, nor is it permitted to become "wallpaper in our home," as Tim Kimmel says. It's easy to use the television as a babysitter when it is the only thing that makes your little one sit still for more than one minute at a time, but television viewing must be monitored and moderated.

Stop reading magazines that breed discontentment. Those magazines that discuss the latest gossip or constantly focus on the outward appearance are not edifying. We become discouraged and depressed, feeling we must go out and buy something in order to try and measure up to the touched-up photographs of models (if marketers have been successful). Cindy Crawford herself said that *she* doesn't even look like Cindy Crawford, so why should we expect that of ourselves?

The Bible tells us that the world *"looks at the outward appearance, but the LORD looks at the heart"* (1 Samuel 16:7). It also tells us that we are wonderfully made (Psalm 139:14) and that we are precious in His sight (Isaiah 43:4). As inspirational author Max Lucado puts it, "If [God] had a wallet, your photo would be in it" (*God Thinks You're Wonderful*). The truth of God's promises and great love for us builds joy in our hearts.

Address the Universal Problem

It is not only the daily distractions in life that we need to remove and approve. If we truly desire a joyful life, we must also consider the removal of heart matters that keep us from experiencing God to the fullest. Allow God to remove your joy-stealing heart matters.

The Bible tells us that we all have a sin problem (Romans 3:23) that keeps us disconnected from God. But there is good news! *"God so loved the world* [that means us] *that he gave his one and only Son, that whoever believes in him shall not perish but have eternal life"* (John 3:16). Anyone can have a whole and lasting life, if only they will confess Jesus as their Lord and believe that He died on the cross to pay the penalty of their sins. It's a free gift (Ephesians 2:8–9). The old is gone and the new will come when you receive Him (2 Corinthians 5:17).

Check Your Heart

To experience more closeness with God, do a heart check. Is there anything holding you back from relating honestly with God? Are you bearing a grudge? Is a refusal to forgive creating a barrier between you and God? Check your heart.

If you need to forgive others, pray this prayer: *"Search me, O God, and know my heart; test me and know my anxious thoughts. See if there is any offensive way in me, and lead me in the way everlasting"* (Psalm 139:23–24). God will reveal to you what in your heart needs to be reconciled. Are you holding on to past hurts? Were you abused? Abandoned? Ridiculed? Rejected? Allow God's incredible love to empower you to forgive. I tell myself, "If God, who is God, can forgive me, just a human sinner, who am I to think that I have the right to hold a grudge against another?" Matthew 6:14 says if we forgive men when they sin against us, our heavenly Father will forgive us.

If you need to forgive yourself, learn to let the past go. After we receive God's forgiveness, we must remember to forgive ourselves. We all have regrets and things in our pasts that we wish we had done differently. We can't change those things now. If God, the all-powerful Creator, can let it go, then we can also; otherwise, we are telling God our standard is higher than His. And when I talk about letting the regretful past go, that includes everything—yes, everything…no exception.

If you need to get proactive, fast and pray. One way to cultivate a close relationship with God is by fasting and prayer. "Fasting is the act of the will through which the follower of Jesus places spiritual control over the flesh (through sacrifice—not eating) with a view toward a more personal and powerful experience with God in prayer," said our pastor, Jeff Warren.

Exercise Self-Discipline and Dependence on God

It takes discipline to remove the daily distractions of time-sucking television, magazines that breed discontentment, and other unedifying home habits, but you can change. However, it takes the power of God to deal with distractions to our hearts. But God tells us in the Bible that we, as followers of Christ, *"can do all things through Christ who strengthens [us]"* (Philippians 4:13 NKJV). A healthy balance of discipline and all-out dependence on Him is the key.

We are urged in the Proverbs to guard our hearts above all else, as they are the wellsprings of life (Proverbs 4:23). A prayer by F. B. Meyer is one of my favorites: "May I not only be delivered from the outward word or action that grieves thee, but may the very springs of my nature be purified."

Remove distractions and see that God approves.

 WHAT NOW, COACH?

- List three steps you will take to minimize the message of the culture and maximize the message of God's truth in your life. Possibilities include disconnect cable TV, have a family commitment to keep TV off for a day or a week, stop taking/buying certain magazines, request to be taken off catalog mailing lists, change the music you listen to, read your Bible daily, and post Scripture throughout your home.

- Whom do you need to forgive? (See Matthew 6:14.) Pray that God will help you forgive that person and gain freedom in that area of your heart. Take a step in that direction by writing a note to God or, if appropriate, a note to the one you are forgiving.

Wanted: Escapee Mom

All moms have full-time jobs, whether they work inside the home only or both outside *and* inside the home.

Someone asked Tony Campolo's wife, Peggy, when she was home full-time with kids, "And what is it that *you* do, my dear?"

She said, "I am socializing two *Homo sapiens* into the dominant values of the Judeo-Christian tradition in order that they might be instruments for the transformation of the social order into the kind of eschatological utopia that God willed from the beginning of creation" (John Ortberg and Ruth Haley Barton, *An Ordinary Day with Jesus*).

Recognizing the Magnitude of the Job

The magnitude of being on call 24 hours a day every day for a myriad of physical, emotional, mental, and spiritual needs can get overwhelming. We must run this mom marathon in a series of sprints, or we may not run strong to the finish. When we are suffering because of "mom overworkia," our families also suffer along with us. You know the saying, "If Momma ain't happy, ain't nobody happy." So many times, that phrase has come to mind when I've been at my wit's end, and then I realize I am setting the tone for the entire family at that moment.

Remove yourself from your role as mom and home manager every now and then, even if it's for only 15 minutes a day. Stop. Really stop.

Recharging

Think about a cell phone. You may have the best that technology has to offer—the sleekest look, multiple features, and the best reception. But after prolonged use with no charging, it won't perform even the simplest of functions. In the same way, you may be the best mom that this world has to offer—the sleekest, with multiple features and great connection—but without charging (no, I'm not talking shopping), you won't be able to perform even the simplest of functions. Take an assessment of yourself today. Are you "out of bars" in any area: physically, mentally, emotionally, or spiritually? What steps can you take to recharge those areas? Quality time with a good friend or sister is one way to recharge emotionally. Positive relationships can boost your energy level like no other thing.

Realistically Recognizing Your Roles

When I had four children, ages seven and younger, I sat in a small discussion group where the question was asked, "How did you serve others during this last week?" I thought and thought, but couldn't remember any time I had ministered. When my turn came, I sadly said, "I can't think of *anyone* I served this week."

A godly older woman gently spoke up and said, "Oh, honey, you are in *full-time* service. That's just about all you *have* done this week."

I have since realized that seemingly insignificant unseen acts performed unto the Lord, such as wiping runny noses, can be more precious to the Lord than the visible ministry positions.

My friend Shannon, mom of multiple little ones, writes down her roles weekly—wife, mom, ministry/outreach leader, home manager, friend, daughter, etc.—and lists responsibilities for the week under those roles.

The purpose of this exercise is to make sure primary roles are covered. When we find ourselves with too many commitments outside our main roles, we're not the only ones who pay the price—our husbands and children do too. We may think, *I just can't say no,* when in reality, we *are* saying no—no to our family. I know there are certain needs only *I* can meet, as they fall under the wife or mom role; those are obviously of vital importance. Minor role tasks are on the second tier; perhaps someone else can lead that ministry project or be the team mom or direct that class.

This prioritizing exercise, along with prayers for wisdom and insight, can help us maintain balance in our lives and correct our efforts in areas we may be neglecting.

Speaking of neglecting, let's talk about the attention we give to our husbands. Do you ever find yourself bending down to tie your husband's shoes (in a double knot), correcting his grammar, or cutting his roast? Our husbands need us to step out of the mom role every once in a while.

The demands on a mother with young children are great. It's easy for a mom to put all her focus and attention on nurturing the children, while the husband stands to the side wondering, *Do I matter anymore? Am I still special, or am I just a paycheck?* While catering to the kids, she neglects to offer her husband the common courtesies she would show for a guest in her home.

Perhaps both the mother and father are forgetting they were first a wife and husband. "With the marriage no longer the focal point of the home, the child becomes the center of their universe as the parents orbit their marriage, their interests, and their schedule around the life of their little one," Ed Young said in *Kid CEO*. He goes on to say, "If your children are taking top tier on the family organizational chart, it's time for you to tell them to clean out their office. You're not firing the children, but you're moving them to the position they should hold."

It's important for me to remember that first and foremost I am a wife to Chris Stull. The children are a welcome addition to the family, but they are *not* the focus of our family. The best gift we can give our children is a strong and secure marriage. When I find I don't have the time to nurture my relationship with Chris, then I know it's time to make a change in my schedule. We need to show our husbands respect and remember that we are not only a mom, but also a friend, companion, and lover to our husbands.

Lover? Yes, it's sometimes more of a challenge to keep this mind-set than others. In my fifth pregnancy, I went through an undesirable phase with each trimester:

- Pimple phase (I suffered the frustrations of adolescence that I had never known.)
- Gray hair phase (Suddenly, gray hairs were appearing every day.)
- Spider vein phase (During this phase, the first thing I did when I woke up was check my legs to see where the newest purple vein had appeared.)

And to "complement" those phases, my belly was growing by the day! It was difficult to feel good about my body when I felt so unattractive.

I know that the combination of sleep deprivation, a postpartum figure, nursing a newborn, and constant demands of other preschoolers doesn't lead to the sexiest thoughts and feelings. Who has time to think beyond survival with so many urgent needs all around? That's when it's time to breathe a "God…help!" prayer. God wants me to love my husband the way he needs to be loved, and He will provide the energy and enthusiasm I need if I offer the willingness.

 ## WHAT NOW, COACH?

- Make a conscious effort to step out of the mom role and be a wife. Start by listing three of the best qualities your husband possesses, and let him know how you feel about those strong qualities.
- List three things you did for your husband while you were dating or were newlyweds that you could still make an effort to do in the coming days to remind him that he is respected and admired. Do each of those things at least one time this week.
- Choose one of these ways to enhance the romance in your marriage:
    - ✓ Post a list for yourself of positive qualities that your husband possesses.
    - ✓ Write a love note to your honey, and hide it in his briefcase.

- ✓ Do whatever it was that you did as newlyweds to express your love and admiration.
- ✓ Compliment him in front of others.
- ✓ Send him an email at the office "just because."
- ✓ Experience the excitement of an affair…a lifelong love affair with your husband.

HAVING A PLACE GIVES YOU SPACE

We have just come through a decade of rental trucks and bassinets. In 12 years, we've moved, had a baby, or moved *and* had a baby nine times. This presents the great challenge of having a place for everything and keeping everything in its place. Since I made my new efficiency resolutions, I've worked regularly in small bits of stolen time to group similar items and assign them to designated places.

Grouping similar items encourages order. If something has a place, it can easily be put away—not only by you, but also other family members. It takes time, but the time you save will greatly outweigh your initial organizing efforts. Strategy number four is having a place gives you space.

APPLICATION

Messy Piles or Setting Up Files?

I have a friend named Suzanne. Name any creative project, and she can do it with flair—sew beautiful pillows, make window treatments, and decorate like a professional. But the details of organizing important papers, such as tax records, insurance, and receipts, are too boring for her attention. There are too many other *fun* things Suzanne would rather be doing. One day, Suzanne came to her wit's end with the stacks of papers, and she stuffed them in an old suitcase in her closet. Whew! Her troubles were out of sight.

Before you go looking for an extra suitcase to make your stacks go away, let's consider a better way. We addressed removing unimportant or unnecessary papers from the house in the last chapter. Now let's talk about what to do with all the papers that you need to *keep*.

A Place for Mail

Assign a central place for opening mail, and keep these items there:

- Letter opener
- Highlighter (to highlight important information)
- Working colored files
- Calendar (to immediately record important dates)
- Phone
- To-do list (to write down RSVPs and other things that require action)

The key is to process the mail *daily*. Having a central place equipped to deal with mail and papers will help you keep control of the mail on a daily basis. When you learn to control your mail, you are taking one big step toward maintaining an orderly house.

Are you completely overwhelmed with stacks of mail from months gone by? The good news is that most of it has expired anyway. You may choose the radical road—free yourself immediately by throwing the stacks away, and starting over with a system in place. Then begin to process your mail *daily*.

As you develop your filing system (as described next), be sure to include a pending folder for mail that needs to be dealt with and paperwork that is in process. Fund-raising papers, memory verse papers, and birthday party invitations that need to be saved for addresses and directions might go in the pending file, keeping stacks of paper off your countertops.

A Filing System

It has always been obvious to me that I need to have a filing system for bills and financial papers. But I didn't think about all the other areas in which files could benefit me. I was able to keep a handle on our home information using folders stashed at different places around the house or in baskets. (I know some of you naturally organized people are gasping right now.) As we added members to our family, I realized a filing system was imperative. Here are some topics I use in my filing system:

- Bank statements
- Car repairs
- Home (general)
- Home improvement information
- Insurance
- Maps
- Medical records
- Miscellaneous coupons (carpet cleaning, dry cleaners, and such)
- Name of each family member
- Receipts
- School information
- Warranty information

What other topics would you need in your filing system? Ask yourself this question: **What is it that makes stacks on my counter or desk? Categorize it, then start a file.** I used to save the grocery ads each week and put them on the counter so they would be handy for checking out the sales. One day I realized that if I continued at this rate, I would have grocery ads on the end of my counter permanently. Every time an ad expired, a new one showed up at my house the next day. I now have a file labeled, "Current grocery ads." Each week when the new ads come, I take out what is in the file and put in the new week's ads. When it's time to go shopping, I can access them immediately.

Make your files work for you and your interests. Organize files in a way that will encourage you to use them, and have files for your interests. Some files that fit my special interests and needs are these:

- **My calligraphy artwork originals:** I can make copies from them.
- **Kids' stickers:** Keep them for projects when the kids need an activity.
- **Home ideas:** Clip ideas, then toss the magazine.
- **Health file for each member of our family:** Jotting down dates of sicknesses and other health-related information could prove to be helpful in the future.
- **Cards to save:** In this file, keep the cards with the rare handwritten message.
- **Drawing lesson plans and ideas:** I reference this file as I prepare to teach summer drawing classes each year.
- **Speech outlines:** I save these for future speaking engagements. I also save anecdotes and stories related to my frequent topics.
- **Kids' extracurricular activity information:** Brochures on tennis camps, gymnastics classes, community center classes, and such go in this one.

Make the files work for you and your personality. Would you do better to have papers filed in notebooks, in a closed drawer, or in an open crate? Although the open crate idea may not win an award for best appearance, it *will* look neater than piles of papers on countertops. Whatever system is easiest for you to process and most likely to be maintained is right for you.

Papers are my greatest organizational challenge. It takes time (and sometimes great emotional effort) to set up a system for the papers in our homes, but it pays great dividends once the system is in place. Remember to break the job down into small parts. Then maintain it by working on it a few minutes every day.

So what became of "Suitcase Suzanne"? She found a solution. Her friend Lisa is great at organizing details but needs help in creative tasks. Suzanne helped Lisa decorate and accessorize her home and, in turn, Lisa helped Suzanne empty the suitcase of papers and set up a filing system. They collaborated to make the most of each other's strengths and get the jobs done.

It takes some time to set up a filing system, but once it is in place, a few minutes each day can keep your papers manageable. Organizational speaker and author Donna Otto says, "Don't pile it; file it!"

 WHAT NOW, COACH?

- Write down your plan for keeping important papers organized. Will you use files or notebooks?
- Get started. Take a pile from your counter, and sort it into categories. File them according to your system.
- Determine your plan for keeping track of bills.

Appointment with the King

Do you desire to know God better? Your schedule will ultimately show if that is a true desire. Are you willing to take steps in the next week to draw closer to Him? The Bible says that if you seek Him with all your heart, you will find Him (Deuteronomy 4:29). Isaiah 43:4 says that you are precious and honored in God's sight and He loves you. The Creator of the universe loves you unconditionally and wants to spend time with you.

Having a place gives you space...for personal spiritual growth. Would you set aside a time and decide on a place to meet with God daily? Most of us think we are too tired and busy. Bible teacher Anne Graham Lotz recently said, "Since I'm always tired and busy, I've decided my prayer life will no longer revolve around my schedule—my schedule will revolve around my prayer life."

Decide on a Place

Ask yourself, "Where would I feel most comfortable for Bible reading and prayer?" Your answer brings you one step closer to implementing a habit of stopping daily to seek to know God better.

My secret to consistent quiet times in the winter months is my space heater. In the winter, the thought of being cold is my greatest detriment to getting up early to read my Bible and pray. It is easier for me to crawl out of my cozy bed when I know that my space heater, set up beside my reading chair, will churn out hot air in a matter of seconds once turned on.

Inspirational speaker and author Jill Briscoe describes a unique place she claimed as her space:

> As a young mother with three preschool children, a husband who traveled, and responsibilities outside the home, I found an unlikely oasis. My children's playpen stood "in the middle of the muddle." So I put the kids out, climbed in, and spent fifteen blissful minutes a day with God. I used that time alone with Him to sort out the muddle and ask Him to help me as a wife and mother be of maximum worth to Him.
>
> After our eldest son was grown, he told me that he and his sister had learned to leave me alone when they saw me in their playpen with my Bible on my lap and a cup of English tea in my hand. "Why was that?" I asked him.
>
> "Because we came to appreciate the fact that you were a whole lot nicer mother when you got out than when you got in," he replied.
>
> —Jill Briscoe, *Daily Study Bible for Women*

Decide on a Daily Time

After 25 years of having a usually regular (but sometimes not-so-regular) time for spiritual growth, I know starting my day with the Lord does wonders for my perspective on the day.

However, you may not be a morning person. I'm not either; my most energetic time is the evening. But I've learned that I'm able to rise much easier in the morning when I get to bed on time.

If I am diligent in my work during the day and consistently find myself staying up until midnight to answer emails and fold laundry, I know it is time to reevaluate the schedule.

"A desire for God which cannot break the chains of sleep is a weak thing and will do but little good for God after it has indulged itself fully," said E. M. Bounds in his book *Power Through Prayer*. I don't know how many days I have awakened to that quote running through my head. (Was that God whispering to me?) How strong is my desire for God? That is a motivating question when it comes to pulling out of bed early in the morning. I once heard Jill Briscoe say, "I'd rather be sleep-deprived than God-deprived."

But moms, please hear this—as each of my five children were newborns, my structured prayer and Bible reading were put on hold for a time. God understands our physical exhaustion and knows our hearts.

Our pastor, Jeff Warren, father of twin girls, says when Whitney and Emily were newborns, he posted on their door this verse from 1 Corinthians 15:51: *"Listen, I tell you a mystery. We will not all sleep, but we will all be changed."* Sound familiar?

During those newborn days, it was all I could do to keep my head above water. Feeding and changing the baby, feeding my family, washing and folding clothes, and working to bring order to the house consumed my days for at least the first six months of the baby's life.

My prayer life was rich as I had plenty of awake time in the middle of the night when everyone else was sleeping. And most of my prayers went like this: "Lord, give me strength. Children are a blessing from the Lord. Pleeeeease help the baby sleep! Children *are* a blessing from the Lord." My Bible reading was hit and miss (mostly miss) in those seasons.

A verse that touched my heart and encouraged me more than any other during those newborn seasons is from Isaiah, and it refs to the Lord as our Shepherd: *"He tends his flock like a shepherd: He gathers the lambs in his arms and carries them close to his heart; he gently leads those that have young"* (Isaiah 40:11). I knew that He was gently leading me with love, understanding, and compassion during those difficult days.

It's Not About Rules, but About Knowing God

Choosing a time and place to meet daily with God is not about rules. It's about the opportunity to know our loving God more intimately. The Bible tells us God's Word is living and active, and God has things to tell us through it. Many times, God's Word gives me specific answers to prayer.

One time God answered directly was when I graduated from college and was job hunting. I was in the final interview for the perfect job, and I was praying the Lord would show me what to do. I was on an emotional roller coaster. *I can't believe that they would consider me, an inexperienced young woman right out of college, for such a job*, I would think. But I was getting married one week after graduation, and this job threatened to cut in on my time of adjustment to marriage and my relationship with Chris. *But the money looks so good! How can I pass this up?*

The morning of my graduation, I opened my one-year Bible to that day's reading: *"Help me to prefer obedience to making money! Turn me away from wanting any other plan than yours"* (Psalm 19:36–37 TLB). It cut to my heart, and I knew at that moment that I could not and would not take the job. *My professors will not understand this; after all, this is what I've studied to do*, I thought. Then I read on: *"How I dread being mocked for obeying, for your laws are right and good. I long to obey them!"* (vv. 39–40). That settled it in my heart—it validated my feeling of dread for disappointing my professors (which was, in reality, probably not a big deal to them anyway). It also made me resolute on my purpose to follow God and trust Him. What a loving Lord He is to so gently guide me!

"At the core of not spending time in the Word is the belief that you don't need Him," inspirational speaker Jennifer Rothschild said at a women's conference I attended a few years ago. Do we dare to believe that without God's help we can be filled with love and joy overflowing and have the strength to meet the challenges and demands of our home and family life?

On a beautiful sunny spring day, my kids and I parked our bikes and ran toward our favorite place on the bike trail near our house. A big swing hangs from a branch in a forest of trees extending 30 to 40 feet above our heads. Two-year-old Karis sat on my lap, and the sun shone down on her face as I pumped us back and forth in the swing. With glee, she tilted her head up and began exclaiming, "I'm pumpin'! I'm pumpin'! I'm pumpin'!"

Just then I realized a tune was going through my head, so I concentrated to hear the words. "Every move I make I make in You, You make me move, Jesus" (David Ruis, "Every Move I Make").

In so many ways, I'm like Karis: her little body could no more make that big swing move than a caterpillar could swing my hanging plant! She was simply sitting on my lap and holding on for the ride. If I sit on my heavenly Father's lap and draw close to Him every day, all I need to do is hold on and He will take care of the rest. This life is just too big to handle for little ol' me. I also know that I need to heed a warning from this object lesson. Just as Karis believed she was the one making things happen, I can slip into falsely believing that I am in control and forget that it is *God* who is in control.

As I relished in the beautiful moment, swinging in the forest, a smile came over my face, and I breathed a silent prayer: "Lord, please help me to always remember that You are the One pumpin'."

 ## WHAT NOW, COACH?

- Pray about having a daily time to meet with the Lord.
  - ✓ Where will your meeting place be, and when?
  - ✓ What devotional book, Bible translation, and journaling notebook will you use?
  - ✓ Give it a try.
- After a week of having a daily quiet time with the Lord, reflect on how it changed you and your outlook.

Kitchen with Kid Strategies

As moms, we spend a lot of time in the kitchen. With little ones around, we need our kitchens to be family friendly and functional. Check out these suggestions:

- **Kitchen toy drawer:** Allot one lower drawer to be used for small toddler toys. It occupies toddlers during that testy dinner-prep hour and also provides them an "acceptable" play drawer to be redirected to when they are trying to get into other cabinets.
- **Baby bottle drawer/bin:** Clear out an easily accessible drawer or bin specifically for the baby's supplies during those months of bottle-feeding. It eliminates the frustration of bottles tipping over in cabinets and small parts getting separated.
- **High location for hazardous cleaners and breakable items:** You know this. Have you done it?
- **Kids' candy bins:** It seems children go from one event to the next, receiving little treats and candies—Christmas to Valentine's Day to Easter, and birthday party treat bags in between! You definitely don't want them downing all the candy in a day or two, yet you don't want the party treat bags sitting on your kitchen counter for weeks, either. One solution is to keep a basket or small bin out of the children's reach in which you store the candy and later ration it out at *your* discretion. (Note: Beware of climbers.)
- **Freezer as storage space:** That's right. Group similar items in open bins to organize.
- **Upper cabinet space for kids' craft items:** Bring down the play dough, paper, and bins of crayons to keep the kids busy while you are cooking in the kitchen.

And, since the kitchen is often the "back foyer," the route used when you leave your home, have a designated place near the door for the following:

- **Hook or basket for car keys:** Be sure to place this out of your toddler's reach.
- **Hooks for items you need when leaving the house:** Your purse, diaper bag, backpacks, and totes are items you might keep on these hooks.

 WHAT NOW, COACH?

- List three changes you can make in your kitchen to make it more family friendly and functional at this stage in your life.
- Make those changes now!

APPLICATION

Stashin' and Storin' Solutions

Having a place gives you space is true also in regard to children's playroom, bedroom, and bathroom storage issues.

Put most of the children's books on a high shelf. Keep within the children's reach a basket or bin with a few books, and rotate in shelved books now and then. If all the books are kept within the toddler's reach, the toddler will pull them all off the shelves, especially when new friends visit. Keeping one basket of books within reach allows small children to still look at books, but makes cleanup time much easier when just a few books have to be picked up.

Store shoes in under-the-bed storage containers on wheels. Are your closets a mess with shoes in the floor? Are you spending too much time looking for the missing shoe? Under-the-bed storage makes it easy for children to store shoes. They just pull out the open container, toss the shoes in, and go. If under-the-bed space is not available, a hanging shoe organizer also works. Store in-season shoes in the lower levels to be within reach.

Have a regular independent playtime for baby and toddler. Yes, this *is* a case of having a place gives you space. It is a time multiplier for the mom and stimulating for the children. Getting them in the habit of playing independently when they are babies is of great benefit to baby and mom.

Factors that contribute to successful independent playtime include five to six favorite toys, classical or fun children's music, and a carefully selected half hour time slot (preferably when children are at their happiest—when they are well rested and have just eaten).

Until they are 16 to 18 months old, they can play in the playpen. After that, if they are ready, they may graduate from playpen play-time to room playtime (same thing, minus the playpen). I like to spice up independent playtime for my children; I've been known to hide a few gummy candies somewhere amidst the toys for them to find during their play. (Candy at 9:00 A.M.? Heaven forbid!) But, as Mary Poppins said, "A spoonful of sugar helps the medicine go down."

Store board games vertically on shelves. When stored that way, a game can be accessed without pulling a whole stack down. Be sure to use strong rubber bands to keep the boxes closed while stored.

Designate one room as a playroom, and keep all toys there. When all toys are kept in one location, bedrooms stay more orderly with only beds, clothes, and a few other items. But few families have the luxury of a playroom. It might be worth putting two small children in one bedroom in order to free a room to use as a playroom. Wherever you decide to keep the toys, use shelves to organize small toy baskets or bins instead of a large toy box, which makes things almost inaccessible. As new toys are added on birthdays and at Christmas, other toys must move out.

Provide a drawer for personal miscellaneous things for each child. This allows them to keep things that are of importance to them without having to clutter the tops of dressers and desks.

Have a basket specifically for library books. They don't need to get mixed in with the family's books. Whenever the library books are not being read, keep them in that basket. Reminders jotted on the calendar tell when books are due. With this system, overdue fines are rare.

Group closet items by subject, season, and color. Store like items together, such as pants and shirts. Keep smaller loose items, such as bags or belts, in bins or baskets.

Prevent lost socks by using sock laundry clips. As dirty socks are slipped off, put them together in a clip. They can run through the washer and dryer, and then be placed back in the drawer still clipped together. No more sock-matching challenges.

Keep a shoe basket near the exit route. This is especially helpful if you have a two-story house. Kids can slip shoes off when they come into the house and put them on as they exit.

Keep socks available on the first level of the house. Again, this applies to a two-story house. Keep socks near the shoe basket. When kids head out the door, they have their socks and shoes right there. We store socks in a chest of drawers near our exit door. In this same chest, we also store often-used items, depending on the season: In the summertime, we store sunglasses and goggles in the drawer; in the winter, we store hats and gloves.

Assign bath towels by color. Assign a different-colored bath towel to each child, and put hooks within their reach to hang towels. We used to have a problem with wet towels in the middle of bedroom floors after bathtime. I was tired of hanging four bath towels every night, so I decided to put four hooks across a long wooden plaque that I painted and hung on the wall within the boys' reach. Each boy has a different-colored towel, all of which bring out the colors in the plaid shower curtain. Now, if someone leaves a towel on the floor, everyone knows whose it is, and that person must assume responsibility to hang it up.

WHAT NOW, COACH?

- Identify one change you can make in your children's bathroom to make it more efficient and useful at this stage in your kids' lives. Now do it.
- Do you like the idea of having a basket for shoes inside the door that is most frequently used when entering and exiting your house? If so, give it a try.
- Do you have a place to stash kids' socks for quick exits? If not, create one.

Setting Up Work Centers

The having a place gives you space strategy applies to grouping in one location everything required to carry out repeated tasks. Setting up work centers greatly increases efficiency.

Work Center Suggestions

- **Mail center:** It is vitally important to have a place to handle mail and papers. Home organizer Kathy Peel calls this "Control Central." It must be an easy-to-access place, so you will be able to supervise children at the same time you deal with daily mail. Have scissors, pens, highlighters, letter opener, calendar, phone, most-used phone books, and working files in that one location (detailed in first application of this section).
- **Phone information center:** Having frequently called numbers stored in your cell phone, including neighbors' home and cell numbers, is helpful. Record frequently called numbers in your organizer that you always keep

with you, or use the computer to print off a list to keep in the car, at work, and various places around the home. A home Rolodex-type system works great for those who like to hold in their hands hard copies of addresses and phone numbers. Each small information card can be added and removed separately from the others. When someone's address changes, you simply make a new card to replace the outdated one.

- **Repair shop:** Having supplies, such as glues, duct tape, and staple gun, grouped in one easily accessible place encourages quick repair of broken items.

- **Mending center:** Keep a bin or basket with sewing basics needed to mend a tear or sew on a button: scissors, needles, thread, seam ripper, and extra buttons.

- **Gift-wrapping center:** If you live in a small home, this probably seems impossible. But a wrapping center simply means having together in one location everything you need to wrap a gift: wrapping paper, gift sacks, tissue paper, tape, scissors, ribbon, tags. If it can be stored near a flat work surface, that is ideal. But your situation might call for an under-the-bed box with a floor to work on. That, too, will do.

- **Hobby items:** Keeping hobby items all together in one location will encourage you to enjoy that hobby with the little snippets of time you can grab. Setup and breakdown time is reduced. With a scrapbooking organizing tote, you can be scrapbooking in less than five minutes.

- **Recipe relief:** How many of those recipes from the newspaper and magazines do you actually copy onto recipe cards? Instead of wasting time copying recipes to go in a recipe file, make a notebook. Use an 8½-by-11-inch three-ring binder with dividers to separate salads, breads, entrées, desserts, etc. Magazine recipes and email recipes from friends can be filed quickly and easily. Clear plastic protectors help keep recipes neat and clean, but are not necessary.

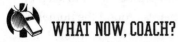

WHAT NOW, COACH?

- Of the work centers just described, identify your greatest needs, and set them up this week.
- Identify a task that you perform on a regular basis. Determine the best place for that task to be carried out and group items needed to perform that task together near that place.

APPLICATION

Money-Saving Storage Solutions

Would you like to be able to access anything you have stored in a matter of minutes? As you start removing and approving in closets and cabinets, you will have things you know you want to keep, but can't decide where to keep them. Let's apply the having a place gives you space strategy to storage box systems.

As I write today, my timer is ticking. In 45 minutes, at the sound of the bell, I will stop writing and start working with my storage boxes, using my last hour of the baby's nap to get a few steps further in swapping out the kids' clothes for the upcoming season.

Storage Box System

- Gather needed equipment and supplies.
  - ✓ Storage boxes: cardboard boxes (file-box sized) or plastic containers
  - ✓ Index card box with multicolored 3-by-5-inch note cards and divider tabs
  - ✓ Marker and ballpoint pen

- Fill each box with related items you want to save. A box the right size to hold files is manageable to work with, move around, and fit into spaces.
- Place a number on the box.
- Write the same number on a 3-by-5-inch card, and record the contents of the box and where the box will be stored. I also like to include how full the box is, in case I want to add similar items in the future. Several times this unpleasant scenario has played out: Someone passes on a few items of clothing to us. I, feeling smug, go to my file to locate that size of clothing…only to go to the box and find it crammed completely full. How discouraging that is! So now I write how full the box is—half full, two-thirds full, or full—at the bottom right of the card so I *know* where that box stands before I *go*.
- File the card numerically under a category (for example, clothes, gifts, decorations, party goods). As we've added more children, I subdivided the clothes category into names. I use pink cards for girl clothes, blue cards for boy clothes, and yellow cards for my things. Not only is that more fun, it helps me get to the card I need quicker.
- Later, as you take something out of a box and put something new in, you simply tear up the old card and make a new one with the same number. This sure beats labeling and relabeling the outside of boxes.

The storage system can also be used for things other than clothes that you want to keep, but don't use regularly. That way, you save your prime real estate—cabinets, dressers, and closets—for things you use often and need to access easily. Consider using storage boxes for these things:
- On-hand baby, wedding, or birthday gifts
- Party goods
- Seasonal decorations
- Miscellaneous electronic items

Changing out clothes for five children and myself is no small job. It's a job I failed, even when I had only two children. I remember my sons being three and two years old when I came across a box in the back of the attic marked "18-month boy clothes." Oops! Derek had totally missed out on a whole box of clothes. Can you imagine the mess I would be in without a storage system now that I have four boys passing down clothes?

I am so thankful for this system mentioned in *The 15-Minute Organizer* by Emilie Barnes and *Get More Done in Less Time* by Donna Otto. It has saved me not only a great deal of time, but also thousands of dollars over the last nine years. The clothes and some shoes have been passed down from one child to the next, so clothing needs have been minimal. Without this system, I know I would either be losing my sanity or having to buy each child a new wardrobe as seasons change. This system helps me lead a life of love toward my family for the glory of God (really).

Oops! There goes my timer. I have all of the kids' winter clothes stacked on tables in their rooms ready to be boxed away. Now I need to go out to the garage and pull out some boxes of summer clothes. Try this having a place gives you space strategy with storage boxes, and it will take only minutes to access anything in storage.

 ## WHAT NOW, COACH?

- Do you need a place to keep infrequently used items (seasonal decorations, kids' out-of-season clothes, party supplies, prepurchased gifts, and such)? Will the numbered storage boxes and card filing system work for you? If yes, decide where you will store the boxes; this will determine the size and type of boxes you will need.
- Buy supplies needed, then get to work clearing out your "prime real estate" areas, so they can be available for frequently used items. Record your progress.
- If you have a system that works better for you, describe it on paper and share that information with other mothers.

Confident Kodak Queen

I used to have photographs scattered all over the house, stashed in whatever drawer or basket that was convenient at the time. That type storage can make scrapbooking a real challenge...and also make drawers and baskets a mess! I've come up with a system for scrapbooking and organizing photographs that works for me:

Scrapbooking

If you have multiple children, organize scrapbooks this way:

- **Children's individual books:** The children's books contain pictures pertinent *primarily* to them (their birth, birthday parties, baptism, class pictures, sports team pictures).
- **Family book:** The family book contains all other pictures that pertain to the family as a whole (family vacation, Christmas, a day at the park, weekend camping trip).

The benefit of having a family book is that you do not have to lay out multiple pages in children's albums for events in which they were all involved. Having multiple albums breaks the project up into manageable bites. You can break it down further by having a family album for Christmas gatherings, vacations, or any other annual picture-taking event.

Whatever your goals may be for saving memories with photographs, come up with a plan and then just do it. Say no to that perfectionist voice. When scrapbooking, ask yourself, "What is my goal? Will I be able to reach that goal if I stew over making the 'best' page? Is a 'good' page OK?"

Organizing and Storing Photographs

New Photographs
- Gather needed equipment:
  - ✓ Plastic file boxes (4-by-6-inch) with dividers
  - ✓ Photo storage box
  - ✓ Pen
- When you get new pictures, pull out your favorite ones to save for albums, and sort them in the 4-by-6 file box under the name of the album they will go in.
- Pull out whatever pictures need to be mailed to grandparents or friends, and put in an envelope with their name and address. Affix a postage stamp immediately.
- File all leftover pictures chronologically in a photo storage box. Label each packet with subject and date on outside, and place negatives in another photo storage box in chronological order.

Past Photographs
- Gather photos and bring them to one area (preferably a large working table).
- Label years on pieces of paper, and lay them out in order on table.
- Set timer for 30 minutes.
- Stack photographs by year. If photos are numerous, use a bin or photo box per year. In the boxes, put dividers for seasons to help sort more chronologically.
- When timer rings, look at the progress you have made. If time allows, reset the timer for another 30 minutes and keep going.
- If photos are grouped in packs, you can then go back and sort somewhat chronologically within the year. If they are loose and all mixed up, pat yourself on the back that you got them sorted by year, and leave it at that.

Digital Photographs

Here is one way to set up digital photo storage without investing in a photo organization software program:

- Create a folder and name it "Photos."
- Create more folders within the Photos folder, and assign a year for each folder name (2007, 2008, 2009).
- Inside each year folder, create month folders (01 January, 02 February, 03 March, etc.). Numbering the months first makes for easier access because the computer will keep them in chronological order rather than alphabetical by month.
- The camera usually assigns digital photos a numeric name based on the date they were taken. Rename favorite photos with the rename function.
- After organizing a hundred or more photos in your photos folder, burn the entire folder onto a CD. Then burn a second copy.
- Store one CD chronologically in your photograph storage box with your prints.
- Print off a proof sheet to use as a reference and store it with the other CD in a notebook with clear sleeves.
- To restore hard-drive space, remove images from your hard drive after burning the CDs.

This should give you an organized method of photograph storage and retrieval and give you backup CDs in case any digital photos get damaged.

Hardest Part Is Done

The biggest challenge in putting a scrapbook or album together is getting the pictures together and in order. As you implement this chronological system, you are done with the hardest part if you decide to make albums in the future. You will free up drawer space, and you'll be able to put your fingers on any picture within minutes. Having a place gives you space...and quick access!

WHAT NOW, COACH?

- Do you have a handle on your photographs? Write out your plan to get organized, and take at least one step toward that plan this week. Hint: If photographs are all over the house, begin by gathering them all together in one location.
- If you also have digital photographs, record how you will keep them (chronological files on your computer or CDs in a notebook).

STRATEGY

HAVE A NOTION ABOUT YOUR MOTION

Do you feel you are rushing around all the time, confused and distracted? My distractibility scale is set at about an eight most of the time! I've always been that way—rushing into a room, only to think, *What was I coming to get?* At least when I was pregnant (a great part of the last 11 years), I could use pregnancy forgetfulness as my excuse. I'm not sure what my excuse is now.

APPLICATION

Scouring Strategies

Think about your movements and steps taken to complete a job. The job we will address first is housecleaning. My favorite slogan the last few years has been Phyllis Diller's statement, "Cleaning your house while your kids are still growing is like shoveling the walk before it stops snowing." Can you relate? Does it frustrate you to rarely see your house clean all at once? Let me share with you a few strategies for having your whole house clean at one time.

Mom's Steps to a Totally Clean House

To get started, gather these supplies:

- A baby stroller loaded with the following:
    - ✓ Cleaning caddy filled with cleaners, brushes, rags, and rubber gloves
    - ✓ Ostrich feather duster (magic at picking up dust, instead of spreading it)
    - ✓ Bag to collect trash
    - ✓ Bag to collect dirty laundry (I like the collapsible mesh carriers.)
    - ✓ Phone and a bottle of water (in case the phone rings or you get thirsty)
- Washtub or laundry basket to use as a temporary bin for belongs-somewhere-else things (items to be deposited when you get to the room where they belong)
- Vacuum cleaner

The steps are easy to remember:

1. Go to one end of the house and completely clean one room and vacuum your way out.
2. Start on the next room.

Keep in mind the rule: **You may not leave a room until it is completely finished.** That's simple enough. As you go to another room, put away from the collection bin anything that belongs there.

Manage Assets Wisely

When housecleaning, capitalize on your strengths. Manage your assets wisely. In other words, do you have children who can help? My typical cleaning day as a mother of children ages one to ten went like this:

- ✓ Hire my eight-year-old or a mother's helper from down the street to watch and play with my baby and three-year-old.

✓ Enlist my oldest child and sometimes my five-year-old to clean. Work together, allowing about five to ten minutes per room. Race the timer to add a little fun.

✓ Start at one end of the house, and work to the other end, room by room, moving the supply stroller and collection bin along with us.

One time Dillon looked up at me in the midst of our cleaning and said, "Mom, I just love cleaning days." I thought to myself, *I'll just enjoy it while it lasts.*

Daily Pickup

On my daily pickup, I go through the same room-by-room routine, making sure beds are made, which immediately gives the room a tidy look, and bringing rooms back to order. I might leave thank-you notes for those who made their beds. Since, as a rule, we bring the house back to order before going to bed, it takes little effort to tidy the house in the mornings. Starting the day with an orderly house is energizing.

I try to never walk empty-handed as I go through the house; of course, babies, instead of stuff, have often filled my arms! If I don't have time to put something away in a room, I at least try to toss it in the appropriate room as I pass by so it will be easier to put away later.

Having a notion about all motions helps keep the house in order.

 WHAT NOW, COACH?

- List ideas to cut down on the number of steps required to clean your house (use cleaner caddy, carry trash bag with you, go from room to room with supply stroller, etc.).
- Who in your household can work alongside you? What can they do (pick up, empty trash, gather laundry, dust)?
- Now, give it a try.

Efficient Kitchen Arrangement

Think about your movements and steps taken to complete a job. One of the hot spots where motion must be addressed and assessed is the kitchen. Wouldn't it be interesting (or depressing) to see how many hours a day we spend in the kitchen?

Cutting Kitchen Steps
Ask yourself, What tasks do I perform in the kitchen? Here are some kitchen tasks to consider:

- ✓ Baking
- ✓ Cooking
- ✓ Preparing baby bottles
- ✓ Making coffee

Then get started organizing for efficiency.

- **Remove the things that do not support tasks carried out in the kitchen.** This takes daily discipline and diligence to maintain, as the kitchen often becomes the family's dumping grounds.
- **Remove duplicates.** Duplicates are necessary only if you use them simultaneously. The larger the item, the more discerning you must be. I own three bread-maker machines, but I run them all at once to bake one large batch on my baking day; so it is efficient for me to have three.
- **Store together the items needed to carry out the tasks.** Ask yourself questions like these: Where do I bake? Are my recipe books easily accessible? Are my measuring cups and spoons close by? Are sugar and flour nearby?
- **Arrange cabinets, keeping hand motion in mind.** Any retrieval that requires more than one movement

discourages you from using that item—especially if you are holding a baby. Cutting down on your movements will cut down on your time and is a key to kitchen efficiency.

"And My God Shall Supply" Aside

And then there are those unexpected times when you have no notion of what motion is going on in your kitchen. I think back to one ordinary day when God orchestrated an extraordinary thing in my kitchen.

Dillon and Derek, ages five and six, put on their favorite baking aprons, and we were ready to begin our bread making. The boys meticulously measured the yeast, flour, sugar, and salt into two bread makers with dreams of the sweet rolls we would enjoy.

I was disappointed when I went to get the oil from the pantry and remembered I was almost out. As I tilted the container, it looked like we had a tablespoon of oil at most. We needed two-thirds of a cup. "Oh no! I'm so sorry, guys! I forgot we were out of oil," I said. "We're not going to be able to finish these recipes today."

Their eyes cast downward. Then my six-year-old looked up and said, "Remember that story about the woman who needed the oil to bake with?"

I took a deep breath and hesitantly said, "In the Bible?" By this time, both boys were excitedly nodding their heads with anticipation. The ball was in my court. "So what you are saying is that we should pray, and the Lord will multiply our oil like He did hers?"

"Yes, yes!" they eagerly and expectantly said.

Almost shaking, I knew I had only one option at that point. We had to pray and ask for God's intervention. As we joined hands around the kitchen bar and I began to speak a feeble prayer, my mind was carrying on another prayer simultaneously: *"Lord, this is **Your** deal. Only **You** can do this. This is **Your** deal. Come through."*

I had a third sphere of thoughts running through my mind on how to explain things to the boys: *God provided us with our neighbor, Saundra, and she is willing to share oil with us from her pantry,* and *God gave us a grocery store just a few blocks away from our house.* I didn't want to bring the prayer to a close, but it was time.

In silence and with all eyes on the measuring cup, I held it (and my breath) over the first bowl and began to pour. To my amazement, it kept pouring and pouring. Again, trying to cover for God, I stopped shy of the one-third cup needed for the first batch, thinking I'd better move to the other batch while the oil was still flowing. I filled a full third of a cup for that batch, then went back and completed the one-third cup for the first batch, which I had slighted.

My boys jumped up and down, gave a high five to each other, and exclaimed, "Yea, God!"

And what about me? I nearly collapsed on the floor, as my eyes filled with tears. "Do you realize what just happened here?" I asked.

Oh, yes, they had. And they weren't surprised—they had expected it.

Though my faith had waned, theirs had been strong. We bowed our heads and thanked God for His supernatural blessing toward us that afternoon. I was *so* grateful that He went out of His way to build the faith of my boys—and myself—that day.

WHAT NOW, COACH?

- Identify one kitchen task you do on a daily basis. Group together in an easily accessible place the things you need to carry out this task.
- Remove five duplicate kitchen items.

Hanging Up the Black-and-White Shirt

I tossed and turned, tossed and turned, sheets sweaty from a long night of disturbing dreams. Then I felt our one-year-old climb into bed with us. I looked at the clock—it was 5:00 A.M. I figured I would let her be, rather than take the risk of being up for the day with her. She coughed and coughed for two hours. By 7:00 A.M. my husband and I dragged ourselves out of bed, even though our bodies wanted to retaliate against the thought. It wasn't just one bad night's sleep. This family of seven was in the middle of an interstate move, and the thousands of decisions and tasks that it demands. We were worn out. But this day was a big day—we would be taking possession of our new house, so we needed to get going.

We dropped the oldest three boys off at school and drove to the title company. For one-and-a-half hours, we signed documents, while unsuccessfully attempting to keep our two preschoolers from crawling under the table, through our legs, and running around the room.

We arrived at the house excited—it was finally ours! The kids ran in as fast as they could and buzzed up the stairs. Chris followed behind them, calling their names, and hit his head on the low-hanging light fixture that would soon have a kitchen table under it. "Bang!" Globes fell and glass shattered all over the brick floor. With no broom or dustpan, we scooped the broken glass up on some title company paperwork and dumped it in the outside trash can.

Just after that, I made a slight movement turning my head and something happened to my back. *Ouch!* My body had succumbed to the torque of my curved spine. Back pain was in order for the day.

Ding-dong. We were encouraged to see three workmen arrive and get to work on some jobs that needed to be done.

However, the chimney sweep, after looking at the situation, delivered bad news: "I can't do it today—don't have the tools I need."

Shortly after he left, we received a call from the painter with a quote twice what we were expecting. As we were trying to assimilate that, the handyman walked up and said, "That will be $500." *For a half a day's work!?!* I thought.

As we were discussing our rising costs, we heard Micah yelling from a bathroom, "I need toilet paper," which our real estate agent, Joan, delivered. Micah went on to say to her, "I need to get my treat for poo-pooing."

We looked up to see a City of McKinney employee, who said, "I'm here to turn your water off."

When I had arranged by phone for all our hookups, they had told me I had to take care of the water in person downtown...and I had forgotten. We pleaded with him for a little grace, promising to go downtown that afternoon.

Meanwhile, the refrigerator delivery was late. Finally, we decided to leave for lunch, but as we were pulling out, the delivery van drove into our cul-de-sac. They unloaded the refrigerator, and as they were driving off, Chris discovered a door was not hanging straight. He called the company. "Your delivery is not registered into the computer yet, but we can bring you another refrigerator in three weeks," they said.

After lunch, while Chris was talking to the painter, Karis came quietly up to Chris and leaned her little head against his leg. Chris reached down to touch her, and when Chris looked at his hand, it was dripping with blood. Karis had been running around our empty house with Micah and had fallen on the one thing that was in the house—the brick fireplace. After calling around and finding out there were no urgent care providers or physicians in our city who could do stitches for her, Chris rushed her to an urgent care 20 miles away. While he did that,

I went downtown to make the water deposit and to the bank to open accounts.

It had been a hot, tiresome day. After school was out for the day and we were back to a full crew, we decided to treat everyone to slushes. We were definitely in need of a pick-me-up. While Chris was changing Karis's diaper, her green slush toppled and spilled all over the carpet. Next, we heard, BANG! Micah wailed, then appeared with a big, purple knot on his head. He had run into a doorknob. Then as we were getting into the car to head back to our temporary home, one of our sons spilled his entire slush all over Chris's floorboard.

When gathered around the table at dinnertime, just after we uttered a pleading prayer of help and thanksgiving for our food, one of our sons spilled his whole glass of milk as "Amen" was spoken. As I rose to get a towel, an unappetizing stench filled my nostrils. It was time to change the baby's diaper.

That night I went to Dillon's room to tuck him into bed and say prayers for him, and as I turned the bedside lamp on, it made a terrible, loud sound. Gray smoke began billowing from it. Thankfully, I was able to unplug it before it went up in flames, but a thick, gray smoke permeated the house. Chris threw open the window, and we were eye-to-eye with a hawk sitting in a tall tree just outside. At this point, feeling we were battling more than just coincidental circumstances, I yelled, "Shut the window before the hawk attacks!"

That night, as we collapsed into bed and recalled the events of the day, I wondered if an appropriate title for my book might be *Living with Hope When You Are Having a Horrible Day*.

Pointers for Dealing with Day-to-Day Roadblocks

Admittedly, some days are harder than others. We especially need to seek God's grace and strength to persevere in those times. But some steps can be taken that will help with common everyday challenges. Have a notion about your motion in your reactions to daily life situations.

Use a Timer. Again, the timer is helpful in keeping homes running smoothly, maintaining fairness, and establishing expectations. It can be used in a variety of ways:

- **Equal time in work:** Set the timer for 5-minute family pickups around the house. *The rule:* Those individuals who are working diligently with a good attitude are done when the timer dings; those who aren't earn more work time.

- **Equal time in play:** Sharing is a hard concept for young preschoolers to understand, but taking turns is easier to grasp. Knowing that when the timer dings in 3 minutes, it will then be their turn to play with the special toy makes it easier to share. This also works with older kids to help them share computer games or a new toy.

- **Homework:** Break down homework time into 15-minute increments. Allow for a play break when the timer sounds. Remember to set the timer for the children to start back on homework.

- **Piano practicing:** Children are sometimes able to focus better during daily instrument practice if they know they will be done when the timer rings. Twenty-five minutes is usually a good time frame for children of early elementary age to practice.

- **Independent playtime:** We discussed in chapter 4 the benefits to both mom and baby for the baby to have some independent time in a playpen. Babies can start at 10 or 15 minutes, but after a few weeks of slowly increasing the time, they can play for 30 minutes a session.

- **Monitoring phone calls:** As a discipline for the caller and the one being called, set the timer for 5 minutes (or whatever time is appropriate) at the beginning of the conversation, and get off the phone when the timer goes off.

- **Potty training:** The timer reminds mom to remind her toddler to go to the bathroom.

Would you like some more ideas?

Create a tattle box. I've hung up the black-and-white striped shirt. Now we have a tattle box. A tattle box is a cardboard box with a slit cut in the top to deposit lists of grievances. The rule is that if it is an emergency, defined as someone bleeding or seriously injured, they may come and tell me. All other problems may be described by words or pictures and deposited in the tattle box for me to read at the end of the day. Though they told their grievances with many words and colorful pictures at first, they quickly figured out it is just easier to work out the problem themselves.

Charge money for mild offenses. The children owe mom money for listening to arguing, whining, or unkind words. My friend Rosalyn marks allowance deductions on the kids' chore charts as offenses are committed. This works especially well for the money-conscious kids.

Anticipate potential problems. Instead of getting frustrated about something that always seems to throw your schedule off at a certain point in your day, expect it to happen and allow time for it. If it doesn't happen, you can rejoice at being ahead of schedule!

At certain times of the day, attitudes tend to be iffy. Pull out fun games or puzzles, or hire a mother's helper to play with the baby or toddler in the afternoon just before dinner.

Plan potty stops while running errands. Take children to the bathroom when it is convenient for you... and hope for few stops in between.

Travel Tips
Traveling with babies and toddlers requires advance planning:
- Allow three days on the front and back side of trips to do everything needed to leave and return home in an organized fashion.
- Keep a packing list on the computer to print off for trips.
- Pack individual bags of snacks and drinks for each person, and let the older ones self-serve.

- Hire a mother's helper or older sibling to play with babies or toddlers the last hour or two before departure so you can focus on packing and loading the car for a trip; a mother's helper is also useful the first hour or two after arrival.
- Keep baby wipes, tissues, paper towels, and a first-aid kit in the car (for long road trips *and* everyday trips).

Know Yourself

It's important to know yourself and make adjustments accordingly.

- Does your license plate read "L8 AGN"? If you are always running late, set your departure time 15 minutes earlier. When departing the house early or on time, it is easier to be patient and understanding with children.
- If a person or situation often upsets you, lower your expectations, focus on the positive, and walk into such situations prayerfully.
- If hormones get the best of you, be aware of your cycle. When possible, plan your most difficult tasks for your best days, and go easy on yourself during PMS.

When it comes to the little things that get you down, be proactive. And the days when the glass globes shatter, your child visits the emergency room, and the hawk is poised to attack, just hold on and pray for strength and steadfastness. Tomorrow will be a new day.

 WHAT NOW, COACH?

- Identify your negative recurring tendencies (running late, can't find your keys). Record your plan(s) to compensate for and correct that tendency.
- List your children's recurring tendencies (fussy in the late afternoon when you are trying to prepare dinner, fighting over a certain toy). Record your plan(s) to anticipate and counteract those negative tendencies.

Exercising Efficient Errands

My friend Denise recently ran a marathon on a Sunday. Monday, she sported bruised heels and injuries to her Achilles tendon. Were the injuries from the marathon? No, she was fine after the marathon. It was the grocery store that did her in. She suffered these injuries the day *after* the marathon while unsuccessfully attempting to dodge the shopping cart pushed by her six-year-old when she took her four children to the grocery store.

Minimizing the hazards and frustrations of errand running takes strategy. Have a notion about your motion as you run errands.

Efficient Errands

- Plan regular anticipated trips.
- Plan your route. Methodically move from one location to the next, preferably in a circle that starts near your house and ends close to your house.

Top Eight Reasons to Run Errands by Yourself

8. Start and complete tasks without a hundred interruptions.
7. Leave baby car seat, toddler toys, juice cups, diaper bag, and snacks at *home*.
6. Make wiser purchasing decisions.
5. Clip through your errands at a quicker pace.
4. Get a break from "mommying."
3. Consolidate your shopping.
2. Decrease your stress level.
1. Have the joy of a grocery cart that still has room in it to put groceries when you begin shopping.

A Plan for the Children

- Hire a babysitter. It will be a great investment in your sanity and your family's sense of order.
- Trade off for child-care services with friends or a family member close by. This is a frugal choice and may help meet another person's needs as well.

If you must take children with you, go to only one or two places at a time. If you must go to more places, take extra snacks and drinks, provide small toys to occupy their attention, and take fun breaks along the way. Pack an extra dose of patience and a lowered set of expectations. And remain aware that potty trainees have a built-in sensor that goes off when they get to the place in the store that is farthest from the bathrooms.

For you, I pray peaceful, productive, joy-filled, and efficient errand days.

 WHAT NOW, COACH?

- Plan an errand day. Determine who will keep the children. List places to go in the order of the most efficient route.
- Identify persons who might be interested in child-care trade-offs for errand day.

APPLICATION

Money in Motion

Does he really expect me to balance the checkbook with each purchase? This right-brained thinker cannot seem to keep up with the record-keeping expectations of her left-brained husband. It's not that I'm clueless. I began working and saving money as a teen and managed to pay for my college education with a few dollars left over. I can be a bit testy when I feel like my purchasing decisions are being scrutinized or criticized.

Many couples are at opposite ends of the spectrum on a lot of things, including the handling of money. Studies show that finances are one of the biggest sources of conflict in a marriage. Most moms are responsible for the majority of their family's nonfixed spending. Communication is key to navigating your way through daily life. Although styles may never be the same, setting financial goals and talking about day-to-day purchases help couples stay on the same page.

Ways to Manage Expenses

These tips for managing expenses may not be pleasant reading for some, but practicing them can relieve stress and bring peace to your heart and home.

Make a budget. Keep track of your expenses for 30 days. Figure your monthly net spendable income and expenses. If expenses exceed your monthly net income, you will need to evaluate your spending.

- **Allow some discretionary dollars each pay period.** You can make fun purchases, knowing you are not robbing from the grocery budget. Spend wisely; once the fun dollars are spent, no more fun spending is allowed until the next pay period.
- **If you don't control your money, it will control you.** As you follow your budget, strive for a balanced perspective—avoid legalism *and* denial.

Lower your standard of living. Face it: Our generation is spoiled. But we can choose not to be. We can change expectations and practice patience.

- **Give yourself wiggle room when purchasing a house.** Think realistically about what you want to spend for a house payment, and don't spend to the maximum of what you qualify for. Financial planners advise purchasing a home only if total housing payments (mortgage, taxes, insurance, utilities, phone, and maintenance) do not exceed 38 percent of net spendable income. A larger house not only costs more in monthly house payment, it costs more in utilities, insurance, taxes, and maintenance.

- **Drive older cars.** Pay cash, or pay off as soon as possible. When you no longer owe money on the car, start making a car payment to yourself every month in savings. This will help you pay cash for your next vehicle. Purchase a newer car if you are spending more on car maintenance than you would on a monthly payment. Before purchasing a used car, have it thoroughly checked out by a mechanic. It is good to have a dependable vehicle for long road trips—security has financial value. If you can't afford to buy a dependable vehicle, rent one for road trips.
- **Buy used furniture or wait** until you can pay cash to completely furnish your home.
- **Seldom eat out.** Generally speaking, it costs at least four times as much to eat out as it does to eat at home. If you have five family members, the cost multiplies exponentially.
- **Forgo entertainment extras,** such as satellite television.

Get out of debt; then stay out of debt. Proverbs 22:7 says, *"The borrower is servant to the lender."* Financial freedom will lower your stress and encourage your marriage. Pay cash and stay ahead. If you choose to have a credit card, stick to one and pay it off each month.

Ways to Stretch Dollars

Let's look at several ways you can make the most of your hard-earned dollars.

Say no to the little extras each day. Dropping your specialty coffee habit could save you $60 a month. Plan ahead and pack snacks and drinks. Forgo the large soda at the drive-through, and drink water.

Plan meals first, then take a list on grocery trips. Buy only items on the list. As previously mentioned, you can probably prepare at least four meals at home for the same cost of eating one meal at a restaurant. Use coupons, ad match, and shop around to get the best value for your food purchases (see chapter 7).

Barter what you have to offer for what you need. I have bartered drawing lessons for the sewing of custom bedding, pillows, and drapes. I have also traded lessons for the making of a video for my husband's fortieth birthday party, child care, meals, painting, and lessons for my own children in other subjects.

Use your local library. Instead of buying books and movies, check them out for free. Take children to free programs. This helps keep your home free of clutter too.

Seek ideas online for making and saving money. Go to *Google.com* to find book exchanges, survey sites to earn money from, money-saving ideas for moms, scrapbook freebies, closeout merchandise, and other topics.

Shop yard sales. You can find used furniture for a fraction of the cost of new. However, when buying baby furniture, be aware of the current safety standards. Here are some purchases I was grateful to find: headboard, $10; vanity chair, $3; antique vanity, $60; four 94-inch custom window treatment panels (just the color I wanted), $5 each; new bar stools, $30 each; cabinet door with cross, free; chair, free; table, $1; chest of drawers, $3; antique dresser, $20; antique mirror, $10; two reading chairs, $10 and $5; new jeans with tags, 25 cents—returned to store for $10 credit; paddles used to hang drapes above window in nautical room, 50 cents each; large oriental rug, $10; custom pillows with fringe, $1 each; and big old square frames, 25 cents each (took pictures out, hung 25-cent wreaths inside, placed on-hand ribbons at top, and positioned them together on the wall—a striking grouping for a total of $1).

Yard Sale Shopping Tips

- Be there early, with cash in hand—plenty of ones, fives, and quarters.
- As you walk up, scan items. Zero in on your most desired items first.
- If you see something you want, pick it up; if it is too large, tell the seller you want it, and set it aside.
- Negotiate. If you would be interested in an item if it were a lower price, it is OK to ask, "What is the lowest you would take for this item?" Or make an offer. Sometimes people have marked things a fair price, but it is not a price that you would pay because your need isn't great enough. It never hurts to say, "I know this is a nice item. I don't need it enough to pay the marked price, but I am willing to pay [$X] for it if you are interested." If they want to just get it out of their house, they might accept your offer.
- Don't buy things for your home just because they are a good deal. Though an item may not cost you much in cash, every item will cost you time and space. Beware of clutter.

Give. Be generous. The most practical thing you can do is give in Jesus's name. Without the grace of God in my life, I'm a total miser. The good gift of frugality can easily sway to the dark side and become a miserly trait without God's help.

As I was growing up, my parents taught me to give, with a thankful heart, 10 percent of whatever I made to the church and to be a good steward of that which God had entrusted me. I worked hard through high school, sometimes cleaning 12 houses a week in the summer to earn money to pay for my college education. I wouldn't spend a dime of it beyond the 10 percent I gave to the church. I would hardly ever buy myself (or anyone else) anything.

Fast-forward ten years. I was mother to two little ones and seeking to make the most of every penny we had. I shopped yard sales for toys and clothes and wouldn't buy items unless I was sure I could resell them at my own yard sale for that amount or more. That can be a wise thing, but for me it was a matter of the heart that had to be dealt with.

At that time, I was meeting weekly in my home with two friends for prayer and to discuss what we were learning from our personal Bible studies. Every week, Kathy brought a big stack of Scriptures from which we would each draw one; then we would read our chosen Scripture aloud.

The first week, I drew out a verse and read it aloud: *"Remember this: Whoever sows sparingly will also reap sparingly, and whoever sows generously will also reap generously.* Second Corinthians 9:6," I read.

The second week I drew out a verse and read it: *"Remember this: Whoever sows sparingly will also reap sparingly, and whoever sows generously will also reap generously.* Second Corinthians 9:6." *Wow, I got that verse last week too,* I thought. *What a coincidence.*

The third week, I reached in the stack of Scriptures to draw a verse, turned it over, and saw that it was the same verse. As my friends waited for me to read it, I said, "It's bad enough when the Lord has to chastise you about something three times in a row. But when He does it in front of others, it's pretty embarrassing." My dear friends prayed with me that I might *get* whatever God was telling me.

Shortly after that, the Lord took Chris and me on a giving journey that we would never have dreamed of. We knew we were just stewards of what He had entrusted to us and had been giving more than our 10 percent—but, of course, the 10 percent had worked on paper. God was calling us to *live by faith* for the first time. We felt He impressed us to substantially increase our giving to a point that no longer worked on paper. We were learning to "give by inspiration instead of calculation," as Chris says.

It's not that God *needs* our money—He owns the whole world and can orchestrate whatever He wills. Our *hearts* are what He needs, and a glance at the checkbook reveals where our hearts are.

Giving does not always work on paper, but it has always worked in real life for us. It is unexplainable. We have always had more than we needed. It seems odd, but giving has been the greatest investment of our money we've ever made.

Do you long for *true* financial freedom? Pray for wisdom, be disciplined with your spending, and trust the divine Giver by giving in Jesus's name. Sow generously and see what you might reap.

 WHAT NOW, COACH?

- Sit down and plan a realistic budget. Don't put it off!
- List three changes you can implement to make better spending choices.
- Identify a local Bible-believing church and some other ministries in which you can invest.
- Pray about your giving. Better yet, commit with your husband to pray one week about your giving, without talking about it. At the end of the week, see if you both feel led to give the same amount. You might be surprised!
- Think about the last time you gave cheerfully and generously. Commit now to doing this again as the Lord gives opportunity.

Organic Teaching

As we begin to have a better notion about our motion in our daily tasks, we must ask ourselves what our motion is teaching our children. Are we frazzled and in a frenzy most of the time, carting them from one event or practice to the next? Do we find ourselves saying, "Hurry, hurry!" repeatedly throughout each day?

We must question ourselves: Are we teaching our children what truly matters and what will extend past our lifetime? Are we teaching them about God and the promises He gives us in His Word as we go through our daily lives?

> *Hear, O Israel: The LORD our God, the LORD is one! You shall love the LORD your God with all your heart, with all your soul, and with all your strength. And these words which I command you today shall be in your heart.* **You shall teach them diligently to your children, and shall talk of them when you sit in your house, when you walk by the way, when you lie down, and when you rise up.** *You shall bind them as a sign on your hand, and they shall be as frontlets between your eyes. You shall write them on the doorposts of your house and on your gates.*
> —Deuteronomy 6:4–9 (NKJV; bold added)

Soul Gardening

My husband and I like to garden. When we lived in Phoenix, each year after Valentine's Day, Chris went to the nursery and bought cilantro, basil, and approximately 30 tomato plants. He tilled the soil and enriched it with compost and potting soil, then carefully set the plants in the fertile ground. We spent the next few months watering and weeding.

We harvested the first tomatoes as a family each year around Memorial Day. One season we charted 275 large tomatoes and estimated we had at least two to three times that number in cherry and yellow pear tomatoes. Friends loved to see us walk into church on Sundays with brown bags of tomatoes to share.

We believe there is hardly any food better than a fresh-picked homegrown tomato. They are not only organic; they are sweet and juicy too. I once heard R. C. Sproul Jr. say on radio that our teaching to our children must be organic. We are *living* textbooks for our children to learn from…every day.

The Bible says that out of the heart springs words and actions (Luke 6:45). When we surrender our hearts to God, He gives us the strength to live a self-controlled and disciplined life. Gossip, exaggeration, white lies, worry, and anger will disappear. The Holy Spirit will produce in our hearts its fruit: *"love, joy, peace, patience, kindness, goodness, faithfulness, gentleness and self-control"* (Galatians 5:22–23).

Around Karis's third birthday, I sang a new song to her at bedtime, and it became a nightly ritual. To the tune of "Frère Jacques," I sang the prayer, "God Our Father," personalizing it for Karis. I sang, "God our Father, God our Father, I thank You, I thank You, for my Karis Joy, for my Karis Joy, Ah-ah-men, Ah-ah-men." One night she chimed in with a grin, "God our Father, God our Father, I ssank You, I ssank You, for my Mommy Joy, for my Mommy Joy, Ah-ah-men, Ah-ah-men." *Am I a mommy joy? Oh, Lord, please help me to be a mommy joy.*

Are you a mommy joy?

Upright actions, attitudes, and words in everyday living teach our children more than we will ever know. Daily life situations provide us with teaching opportunities. When we are driving and see an ambulance, I lead the children right then in prayer for whoever is in trouble and in special need of God's help. And if I forget, my kids remind me. This not only helps the one in trouble, as we lift them up in prayer, but teaches my children to call on the name of the Lord in time of need. It teaches them to have faith that our prayers really do make a difference and to be aware of those around us who may need a prayer on their behalf.

What Is It Worth to You?

A friend of mine recently accompanied a group of Girl Scouts to Disneyland. When they got to one of the more popular rides, they were frustrated with the long line. My friend was disheartened as one of the other adult leaders told her daughter to lie about having an express pass like her friends so they would all be able to move to the short line. She sacrificed a lifetime lesson in the important character quality of integrity for the sake of saving 45 minutes.

My friend Jeanie recalls a lesson her husband, Larry, taught their son. Larry and their son, who had just turned 13, went to a car show. The price was $15 for adults and $7 for children ages 12 and under. Dismayed at the difference in price, Larry still paid it. Later his son said that made a huge impact on him—a positive lesson in integrity. That was eight dollars well spent.

 WHAT NOW, COACH?

- Recall some times you, in the presence of your children, have chosen integrity over cost or convenience.
- List changes you can make in each of the following areas in order to be a better example to your children:
  - ✓ Actions
  - ✓ Attitudes
  - ✓ Words

Meaningful Family Rituals

It's easy to get on the fast track of life and speed through without thinking about meaningful ways in which we might teach our children today the values and beliefs that are most important to us.

Importance of Family Rituals

Another word for family ritual is *tradition.* That word conjures up mixed feelings and emotions. "I don't want my religion to be just a tradition; I want it to be a real and personal relationship with God," one might say. That person wants to know that there is a real meaning behind religious traditions. Or another might complacently remark, "I have no idea *why* we do it this way; it's just a tradition," as they go through the motions.

Regardless of the negative connotation the word *tradition* has taken on, traditions can be powerful teaching tools in our families, allowing us to show our children, in concrete ways, what really matters most to us.

Examples of Family Rituals

- **Starting and ending each day with "I love you's" and big hugs**
- **Singing a special song in the morning or at bedtime**
- **Bedtime prayers and back scratches**
    My dad was the best at this.
- **Attending church regularly**
    This teaches children the importance of regularly meeting together with believers to worship God, learn more about Him, and fellowship. Aside from providing spiritual benefits, regular church attendance is also apparently associated with health benefits. My doctor told me a recent study showed that people who go to church regularly have improved health and fewer doctor visits.
- **Eating dinner together**
    This shows family time is valued.
- **Thanking God before meals**
    This teaches our children to recognize and show gratefulness toward our Maker and all-powerful Provider for meeting our needs.
- **A special plate, cup, glass, or other item for celebrating family members' accomplishments (big or small)**
- **A certain food everyone loves**
    Serve it at your family's special occasions.
- **Special children's activities during the holidays that define who we are and why we are here**

- **Christmas celebration**

  Enjoy the decorations, Advent calendar, and candle-light service. Make a birthday cake for Jesus. Have kids act out Nativity.
- **Easter celebration**

  Resurrection eggs share the Easter story. Serve Resurrection cookies, and host a neighborhood egg hunt.

Simplifying and striving to be realistic about expectations and commitments during the holidays help us to be joyful in the midst of hosting family celebrations.

 WHAT NOW, COACH?

- List three current family rituals you are practicing to teach your children in concrete ways what matters most to you.
- List three new ideas for family rituals and the values that each could teach. Try at least one of the rituals this week.
- Ask your husband to travel down memory lane, and record two to three of your husband's favorite childhood rituals. If you are not married, ask a friend to share childhood ritual memories. Adopt one of these rituals as a new one for your family.

TWO FOR ONES ARE SO MUCH FUN

Do you love two-for-the-price-of-one sales? The thrill of the deal is exhilarating! I recently heard someone say, "Men will pay two dollars for a one-dollar item that they need. Women will pay one dollar for a two-dollar item they *don't* need." Let's talk about task two for ones—getting two things accomplished in the process of doing one task.

APPLICATION

Cut Your Kitchen Time

Walk with me to the room where family life revolves each day. Do you hear the crackling of sautéed onions and peppers in the skillet and smell the brownies baking in the oven? Sit down with me, and let's enjoy a mug of freshly brewed hot coffee in the kitchen as we discuss making the most of food preparation efforts.

Lunch Box Solutions

Would you like to reduce school-morning stress? Then try making all the sandwiches for the week at one time.

Steps

1. Deal out slices of bread on a cutting board or cookie sheet.
2. Spread on mayonnaise and mustard or peanut butter and jelly with a large icing spreader.
3. Add lunch meat or cheese as needed.
4. Place sandwiches in plastic sandwich bags.
5. Write on the bag with a permanent marker either the name of the child or the type of sandwich.
6. Place sandwiches in a bin or door pocket of the freezer.
7. Pull out sandwiches as needed each morning to pack lunch boxes.

Tips

- Peanut butter and jelly, bread, and lunch meat all freeze fine. They thaw in the lunch box and are ready to eat by lunchtime.
- Don't freeze garnishes, such as lettuce, tomato, and pickles.
- Don't wait until you are in a jam to spread the jam. Pick an unhurried time to make the sandwiches—perhaps over the weekend.
- Once-a-week sandwich making saves time, as only one setup and one cleanup are required.
- Save even more time by involving the kids. When they are old enough to handle the job (between ages eight and ten), set the ingredients out and let them make their own sandwiches.
- Bag other lunch box foods, such as pretzels, carrot sticks, and cookies, at the same time. This will save you even more time on school mornings.
- Fill a durable water bottle one-third full of water, and place it in a tilted position in the freezer to freeze overnight. In the morning, fill the bottle with water and pack.

Using these tips, you will find school mornings much less stressful. Put the following in a lunch bag and the lunches are ready to go:

- ✓ Sandwich (from freezer)
- ✓ Pretzels or chips (from freezer)
- ✓ A piece of fruit
- ✓ Carrot sticks (from refrigerator)
- ✓ Dessert
- ✓ Drink

This *pre*preparation will boost your energy and morale in the mornings by at least 100 percent...guaranteed.

Snack Solutions

Make (or buy) big batches of trail mix; then distribute the mix into individual-serving snack baggies and store them in bins. Children can grab a bag to curb hunger pangs at home or in the car.

> *Fewer fast-food restaurant stops =*
> *saved time + saved money + better nutrition*

One of the most useful and creative gifts I received after having my fourth baby was a big box of bagged healthy snacks for the children. My friend Leah brought individual portions of trail mix, crackers, dried fruit, 100 percent fruit roll ups, and nuts. When a child said, "Mommy, I'm hungry," and I was busy nursing the baby, I simply said, "Go pick a snack. They are in a bin on the lowest shelf in the pantry."

When taking long car trips, it is helpful to give all the children their own snack bag complete with snacks and drink. Gallon-size clear plastic bags labeled with names work well.

Other Kitchen Two for Ones

Buy food in large quantities and divide ahead of time in order to save time in the future:

- Grill extra chicken, dice it, and bag it to use in recipes as needed. Remember to label bag with contents and date.
- Brown extra ground beef and bag in one-pound portions.
- Buy bagels and slice and freeze them immediately. Pull them out the night before or even the morning of use. Bread thaws quickly. After toasting, they are scrumptious. Note: Try to use bread within a week or two of putting it in freezer, so it won't get freezer burn.
- Shred cheese, divide into quart-size freezer bags, label, then freeze.
- Double recipes when you cook, and freeze the extra. Always label with contents and date. Pull a frozen batch out the night before a busy day, and keep it in the refrigerator to be warmed for dinner.
- If you like to make home-baked cookies, make extra cookie dough and roll into balls and freeze. As you prepare dinner, pull out what you need, thaw, and then pop them in the oven. You'll have warm, home-baked cookies for dessert. Yum! Faster yet, purchase a tub of cookie dough at the store, and do the same.
- Bag ice ahead of time when you know you will be hosting people in your home.

Kitchen two-for-one possibilities are endless, depending on what foods you use most regularly.

Keys to Success
- Clearly label food that is going into the freezer: Record the contents, amount, and date.
- Treat the freezer as another space to be organized. Group like things together and use shoebox-size clear bins for bagged items.
- An extra freezer or refrigerator encourages family two for ones. The extra cold storage makes room for multiple gallons of milk, dozens of eggs, drinks, and produce, reducing the number of grocery store trips required.

Two-for-One Baking

Before we leave the kitchen, I want to share a favorite baking two for one. My mom and grandma always made beautiful homemade cinnamon roll rings for Christmas, Thanksgiving, and other special occasions. With the invention of bread makers in the 1990s, I began carrying on the tradition.

When I make cinnamon roll rings, it's a long, messy process; so when I have a baking day, I make lots. Flour is flying that day. In less than seven minutes, I can have three bread makers humming, which will yield about eight rings. As events, birthdays, and needs come up through the week, I am prepared with a special home-baked gift.

What does this recipe for kitchen two for ones yield? For me, close to 100 cinnamon roll rings a year—but best of all, saved time and energy...and big smiles on the faces of the cook and her family!

 WHAT NOW, COACH?

- List three changes you will make to be more efficient with kitchen tasks this week.
- Identify several favorite family recipes that can be cooked in batches and frozen.

APPLICATION
37

See Multiple Results

My son Dillon is a math whiz. I've always called his dad the Walking Calculator, and now we have Walking Calculator Jr. When Dillon was in the sixth grade, he came up with a new math theorem while sitting in class one day. His fun spring break project that year was proving that his math theorem always works, no matter what number one begins with. He taped together sheets of paper—seven wide and seven deep—to work his proof. It always ended with a zero on top. This theorem is called the Stull Pyramid—watch for it in future math textbooks! Dillon knows about multiplication.

I may not understand many math theories and may not be able to multiply as quickly as my math whizzes, but I do know that piggybacking activities makes a great two for one. Getting two or more things done at the same time with just one setup and one cleanup is the aim.

This can be especially helpful during high-stress seasons. In December, the flickering lights, beautiful music, and tastes of once-a-year treats are all reminders of the eternal joy we have because of Christ's birth. But for moms, this wonderful season can be the most stressful time of the year.

Get-It-Done Christmas Gift Wrapping

1. Make a gift list, buy gifts early, and store all the gifts in one location.
2. Set up an extra table in a room or the garage.
3. Gather Christmas wrapping paper, bags, tissue paper, tape, scissors, ribbon and bows, labels, pen, and trash can—all to be placed within easy reach.
4. Lay out gifts on table.
5. Label each gift with a sticky note that indicates the recipient's name.
6. Set the timer for 30 minutes or one hour.
7. Wrap as fast as you can until timer rings.
8. Repeat steps 6 through 7 until you can move to step 9.
9. When all gifts are wrapped, put a big check on your to-do list and enjoy the season.

Having a place to store prepurchased gifts throughout the year is essential to this process. Trying to conceal family members' Christmas gifts can get tricky, especially if gifts are stashed in multiple locations. A mysterious note on the calendar at the beginning of December can remind moms where Christmas gifts are hidden.

Ironing

The next topic is one of my most dreaded chores: ironing. Ironing regularly all at once before putting clothes away can make it bearable. One setup and one cleanup, and the ironing is done. No more stressed-out ironing in the morning before walking out the door!

But here is my best tip: **Whenever possible, avoid ironing altogether!**

- Buy clothing made of blended fabrics. They are less likely to need ironing than 100 percent cotton clothes. When buying, count the cost not only in price but in the time it will take to maintain.
- Remove clothes from the dryer when they are slightly damp; hand press, and then hang.
- Lay out children's clothes on the floor the night before, spray wrinkles with a water spray bottle, and hand press.
- Adjust your budget and delegate to your local dry cleaner the cleaning and ironing of men's dress shirts (less than two dollars per shirt—well worth it).

A few months ago, I had a number of pieces to iron one evening and was standing at the ironing board having a pity party. A tune kept running over and over through my head. Finally, I thought, *What is this song I keep hearing?* Then some of the words came to me: "Dear Lord, with the prize clear before our eyes, we find the strength to press on" ("Press On," written by Dan Burgess, sung by Selah). I laughed out loud! God is so funny sometimes. I knew He would strengthen me for every good work He had for me to do as I served my family...and I *could* press on!

WHAT NOW, COACH?

- What activities can you piggyback? The goal is to get two or more things done with only one setup and cleanup.
- What messy chore can you combine with outside play for one cleanup? For example, could you water the garden or wash the car while your children run through the water in their swimsuits?

APPLICATION

38

Confessions of a Biker Mom

"My tire's out of air." "I can't find my helmet." "Where is the dog's leash?" "I forgot my water bottle." "The baby spilled her Cheerios." "I need to run in and grab my sunglasses." Sometimes the preparation for a family biking trip takes longer than the trip itself.

Exercising with Children
When you pack some extra patience and lowered expectations, exercising with children has many benefits—ranking it better than a two-for-one deal.

- Spend quality time with your kids and get exercise at the same time.
- Exercise while the baby is awake, and use naptime for other activities and tasks.
- See some sites, get fresh air, and take in the sunshine.
- Keep your energetic one-year-old out of trouble for a half hour as the little one is strapped safely in place.
- Model physical fitness to your children.

The type of exercise you can get with children changes with their ages. Preschoolers can ride bikes with training wheels or a tricycle while you walk, pushing a stroller. When they are ready to drop the training wheels, get ready to get that heart rate up as you run to keep up with them! The next step is biking along with them.

If you have a gym with good child care nearby, you might choose to exercise and get some time to yourself at the same time. As I finished the rewrites on my manuscript for this book, I visited the gym frequently. My kids loved the Kids Club with its large indoor playground, dollhouse, computer games, and art activities. Meanwhile, with notebook and pen in hand, I walked and worked in my private bubble amidst the hum of whirring treadmills. (I don't think very well sitting still anyway.) How long did it take to edit a chapter? About six miles.

An Exercise of Kindness

How about exercise of the ministry kind? Involve your children in serving others alongside you, and you will see exponential results.

One day when Dillon and Derek were preschoolers, I was talking to them about kindness. My thoughts and prayer that day were on this line: *One thing we could do to show kindness and love is visit the elderly at a nursing home, but I don't know anything about any nursing homes around here. Lord, please show me what to do.*

A few days later, I was in the shower when three words ran over and over through my head: *Scottsdale Heritage Court...Scottsdale Heritage Court...Scottsdale Heritage Court. What in the world is Scottsdale Heritage Court?* I thought. Then it hit me. *Could this be an answer to my prayer?*

I quickly rinsed the shampoo from my hair, dried off, dressed, and scurried to the kitchen to grab the phone book. There it was, plain and clear: Scottsdale Heritage Court. When I saw the address, I noted it was less than a mile from my house. Trembling, I called the number.

"Scottsdale Heritage Court. How may I help you?"

"Is this a nursing home?" I asked.

"Yes, it is."

"I need to know your visiting hours."

The next night at prayer meeting, we were praying for the sick and homebound members of our church. Listed under nursing homes was Scottsdale Heritage Court and the name of a woman from our church, Oleta.

The very next day, we went to visit Oleta. We learned that her family lived out of state, and she rarely had visitors. We began to go see Oleta weekly; we took our small gifts of hugs, cookies, and pictures the boys drew.

One Wednesday night in prayer meeting, they shared that Oleta had gone on to be with the Lord. I thank God that my boys and I were a part of a special ministry of love and kindness to Oleta her last weeks on earth.

In what ministries can you involve your children?

Check out some of these opportunities through which your children can experience ministry:

- Gather canned foods for a community food pantry.
- Take the school crossing guard a cup of hot chocolate on a cold day.
- In place of a gift for the birthday child, ask friends to bring new or gently used books to donate to a library or hospital.
- Host a neighborhood Bible club for kids.
- Sponsor a Third World child monthly; keep the child's photo on your refrigerator and pray as a family for the child; let the kids pool their allowance money to send an extra financial gift to that child at Christmastime.
- Help serve homeless people Thanksgiving dinner.
- Help elderly neighbors by pulling weeds from their flower beds.
- Pull your neighbors' trash cans from the curb back to their houses.

All of these things, done with your children and in the name of Jesus, have a powerful effect—exponential, in fact.

WHAT NOW, COACH?

- What activity can you do with your children for exercise?
- Identify a ministry service you can exercise (do) with your children.

 APPLICATION

Volunteerism by Violations

Do you want to better your house *and* children at the same time? Have them "pay off" mild offenses with household chores. Putting children to work can bring a stop to whining, teasing, and rejoicing in another's failure. Now that's a good two for one.

How Does Volunteerism by Violation Work?

When your child commits a mild offense, say, "Thank you for volunteering to [name a chore of your choice: carry out the trash, gather the laundry, do a five-minute pickup]."

- If attitude wavers, say, "Is that a complaint?" (I learned this one from my mom.) This gives them a little grace to straighten up and obey.
- If the chore is done with a good attitude, they are done when the task is complete.
- If chore is performed without a good attitude, it does not count as payoff. Go back to the beginning.

Remember these key points that help with attitudes but, in turn, cut back on the number of "volunteers by violation":

- Lay down the rules in the beginning. Tell your children what you expect them to do and when and how you expect them to do it.

- Remind them that the ball is in their court. "You may either make a decision to behave today and have only one chore or make a choice not to behave and help around the house all day."
- Be consistent.
- If you have extra jobs that need to be done on a certain day, watch for "volunteer opportunities." Give the children fair warning that you will be especially on the alert for bad attitudes, teasing, or whining, as you are in need of volunteers for extra jobs that day.

The Violation of Out-of-Place Items

Here's another two for one that teaches responsibility to your children and betters your house at the same time. When children's things are scattered about the house, carry out these steps:
- Give a warning that in ten minutes you will be collecting out-of-place items.
- After ten minutes, collect items in a box.
- Children must do a chore to earn back their items from the box.
- All unclaimed items get donated to charity. (This also helps declutter the house.)

Let's all say this together...

*When Momma doesn't have to go past step one,
two for ones are so much fun!*

 WHAT NOW, COACH?

- Tell your children your expectations. Then try out volunteerism by violations.
- When your child commits an offense, respond by saying, "Thank you for volunteering to _____."

- Remember, completing a chore will be counted as payoff only if it is done with a good attitude.
- Record the offense and your child's response to this type of discipline.

APPLICATION

40

Instructing While Stressed

All children have their own personality and their own God-given strengths and weaknesses. The more children we have had, the more I've understood this to be true. We have been amazed as we have noted the uniqueness of each child God has added to our team. We must take the time to understand our children's God-given personalities and pray for wisdom in the best way to teach and train each one.

Making Amends

One of our children has a harder time sitting still than the others. He has been that way since he was a baby. Instead of doing something quiet, like sitting and reading, he would much rather be in the middle of all the action—dressing up in costumes, interacting with others, singing, and dancing. You'll not find a heart any bigger than his when it comes to loving people. He's one of the greatest encouragers I know—everybody's best friend. And his schoolteachers tell me they've never seen a happier child.

But this happy, playful child still must do homework, study for tests, and perform other tasks that require mental diligence and focus. Please do not misunderstand—the boy practically aced the cognitive abilities test. He has brains. Trying to help him transfer that intelligence into diligence with his studies was an activity that stirred up frustration in me almost daily when he was in early elementary school.

One afternoon, I was trying to help him study for a spelling test. He wouldn't sit still long enough to get through one word, much less a dozen. I had a newborn to feed and three other children's needs to attend to. I came to the end of my patience after an hour and a half and shouted angrily, "You are going to sit in this seat until you have every one of these words learned!" I looked into his eyes and knew I had crossed the line. Children can tell the difference between times we are disciplining them in love for their own good and times we're attacking them as a person. With so much to do in preparation for church activities that night, I dropped the task in a huff and went on to serve dinner.

That night at church, I was voicing my frustrations to another mother. Knowing that child's creative personality type, she suggested we play active games, such as hangman, to learn the spelling words. Knowing how much he loves to draw, I took it a step further: If he created pictures to remind him of how the words were spelled, he would have it.

After getting home that night and running children through baths or showers and brushing teeth, I asked this son to meet me in the living room instead of heading to bed. As I came in to sit and was going to tell him this great idea for his studies, bless his loving heart, he immediately said, "It's OK, Mom. It's OK." And he gave me a huge hug.

Oh, was it that bad? I thought. I had snapped at him earlier in anger, and he knew an apology was due. And I knew I must make my apology. He needed to hear from me those words that are so difficult to say: "I was wrong." It wouldn't have been enough for me to say, "I'm sorry you felt that way"—that would not have addressed my failings. Without making excuses (though it was very hard), I said, "I was wrong. Please forgive me." And of course, he already had.

We then talked about how I was more than willing to offer help if he was willing to try and agreed that we would try some creative study options. Our study frustrations were not completely over, but he did begin learning his spelling words more quickly and enjoyably.

Mending the Hurt, Modeling Humility

When we take the step to admit our faults and ask forgiveness from our children, it is a powerful thing. We are not only mending the hurt in that relationship but also modeling humility to them. We may take that moment to teach them that God is the only One who will never let them down and encourage them to trust their loving Creator with all that they are. Though my moods shift, the Bible tells us that Jesus, our Savior, is *"the same yesterday and today and forever"* (Hebrews 13:8), and that the Lord is *"faithful to all his promises and loving toward all he has made"* (Psalm 145:13).

You may have many regrets for the way you have treated your children from time to time. Write them down and confess these things to your children today in words they can understand. Start with a clean slate, and see what happens in your relationship and in the spirit of your children.

Guarding the Hearts of Children

The Bible tells us that the heart *"is the wellspring of life"* (Proverbs 4:23), and it must be guarded above all things, so do not neglect your part in the housekeeping of your child's heart. This two for one may not sound like a lot of fun, but it does wonders to strengthen our relationships with our children *and* our children's faith in God.

 WHAT NOW, COACH?

- Relating to some wrong you did in the recent past or a failure this week, say to your child the difficult words, "I was wrong."
- Note how your child responds.

Conversations with God
(And Young Eavesdroppers)

Micah recently received three immunizations in his legs. That evening, as he was stepping into the bath, he asked, "If I take these Band-Aids off, will it let water in the holes?" You might laugh, but that was a valid question for a child.

Let's talk about something that *can* seep deep inside our children—into their hearts and souls: faith in God and the belief in the power of prayer.

The Power of Prayertime with Children

One of my most special daily times with my children is at night just before they go to sleep. I kneel beside their beds, we exchange a few thoughts on the day by the glow of a night-light, and then they know they can count on a prayer on their behalf. The words, intertwined with back scratches and then hugs and kisses afterwards, are lifted up to God.

This two for one is not just fun—it's knock-your-socks-off powerful. God is listening, and the prayers *will* be answered (1 John 5:14–15). Not only that, but the children are listening also. They're affirmed in who they are, and our relationship is strengthened. They are also learning the importance of prayer and daily dependence on God.

Praying for Your Child

- Thank God for how special He made your child—noting there is no one else in the whole world just like him or her (biblical self-esteem). *"I praise you because I am fearfully and wonderfully made"* (Psalm 139:14).
- Thank God that you have the privilege of being his or her mom.

- Ask God to send angels to watch over your child through the night and the next day (protection). *"For he will command his angels concerning you to guard you in all your ways"* (Psalm 91:11).
- Ask God to guard your child's heart and mind in Christ Jesus. *"And the peace of God, which transcends all understanding, will guard your hearts and your minds in Christ Jesus"* (Philippians 4:7).
- Pray for needs of teachers and friends (teaching your child to intercede for others).
- Thank God for a special incident in which your child displayed a positive character quality (honesty, patience, generosity, kindness, self-control, gratefulness, diligence, obedience, gentleness, joyfulness, or orderliness).
- Pray for God to help your child in an area of character that needs to be developed.
- Thank God for the plans He has for that child. *"'For I know the plans I have for you,' declares the* LORD, *'plans to prosper you and not to harm you, plans to give you hope and a future'"* (Jeremiah 29:11).

In praying this way, your child and your relationship with that child are affirmed and strengthened, the child learns the importance of prayer and daily dependence on God, and God is listening...and will answer.

Prayertime Techniques

Chris and I work as a tag team, taking turns saying prayers for the children at bedtime. Some nights, I can muster only enough energy for an "I love you" and a short prayer with each of the children. The older children sometimes come in to ask me questions about their homework as I'm praying with the younger ones; other times, I'm telling one child to pick up his dirty laundry off the floor in one breath, then finishing the prayer with another. Do not wait for a perfect setting for prayer—just do it.

Another tip that will help is to stick with a regular and early bedtime. Studies are showing that children are not getting enough sleep these days, and many believe that problems like attention deficit disorder are directly linked to lack of sleep. According to Mary Sheedy Kurcinka (*Sleepless in America*), kids need the following amounts of sleep over 24 hours:

Infants (0–12 months)	14–18 hours
Toddlers (13–36 months)	13 hours (including naps)
Preschoolers (37–60 months)	12 hours (including naps)
School-age children (6–12 years)	10–11 hours
Adolescents (13–19 years)	9.25 hours

Put the youngest ones to bed first, and allow the older kids to read before lights-out if they are not sleepy yet.

A recent report said that a husband and wife with three children typically communicate about 12 minutes a day. Putting the children to bed early will not only improve the prayertime process, it will free up some time for you to communicate with your spouse.

SOS Prayers

I have to admit that besides bedtimes and meals, the other times my kids most often hear me pray out loud is when I'm losing my patience with them! In *What Happens When Women Pray*, Evelyn Christenson talks about SOS prayers. Those are quick prayers we lift up to God in our minds when we are having a hard time dealing with someone. We are saying: "SOS, Lord. Give me Your attitude toward this person."

Evelyn talks about how God will always answer yes to an SOS prayer, because it is *always* His will that we have His attitude toward those around us.

I often lift up those SOS prayers out loud to the Lord in front of my children. (I figure that is a better alternative to wringing their necks.) In those times, not only does God's power and wisdom come through, but also our children realize at least two things:

1. Prayer is important and can take place anywhere.
2. Mom is dependent upon God to stay self-controlled.

"Presents" from God

"Mom, God gave me lots of presents," four-year-old Micah said one day.

"God gave you lots of presents?" I asked, trying to think of what toys he was referring to.

"He gave me fast legs to run, and I am a good organizer."

Oh, gifts. "Yes, Micah, He *has* given you lots of presents."

What presents has God given *your* children? Have they heard you thank God for them? You've got tonight.

 WHAT NOW, COACH?

- Practice the nightly ritual of praying for your children when you tuck them into bed.
- Think of prayer points you could add to the list provided in this chapter.
- Record your thoughts on how prayertime with the children went.

APPLICATION

Entrepreneur Encounters

Would you like to teach your children a new skill and get paid for it? What skills do you have that you have intended to pass on to your children, but, because you have had no plan for it, you haven't done it yet? Start a class, and you'll be sure to get it done.

What could you teach? Manners, arts and crafts, piano, cooking, music, swimming, painting, jump rope, or drawing?

Parents of young children are eager to find enriching activities for their children to be involved in on long summer days. If you offer a class at your house, your neighbors will probably be interested. They won't even have to get in the car to participate.

Offering a Class in Your Home

Hosting classes in your home has several advantages:

- You do not have to load everyone in a car and travel to another place.
- You do not have to pay a room fee. The only cost is the effort it takes you to clean your house—which needs to be done anyway.
- You can teach during your baby's naptime.
- You may offer snacktime, and pull out the snacks you have on hand—even frozen treats.
- Your children participate for free.
- You are accountable to reach your goals of teaching these skills to your children.

When holding classes in your home, you must be extra diligent in your professionalism:

- Research fees charged for similar classes, and offer your class for at least half price since it is in your home. If you are new in the field, reduce further until you gain experience.
- Create flyers that include all pertinent details: description of course, days offered, eligible age group, location, times, cost, supply list, and benefits of taking the class. Sending flyers by email encourages moms to forward to other moms who might be interested.
- Dress professionally, as you would in a classroom.
- Invest in some folding tables and chairs if needed.
- Invest in a chalkboard or other needed supplies.
- Communicate clearly to the children how you expect them to behave.
- Be well prepared with your curriculum.

- Gather all class fees by the first class.
- Start on time and end on time.

You may think you cannot do this, but you can. Talk to neighbors and friends. Moms are the best at passing on good information. If you offer the class, "they will come." Your classes will fill up quickly.

My friend Lesley ran Camp Promise in her home one summer. She had a three-year-old and a five-year-old, so she did camps for those ages. She did creative and fun hands-on activities with the kids to teach them about Jesus. It was a three- or five-day week at an affordable price. My two preschoolers participated. They enjoyed interacting with kids their age, loved the crafts, and learned much about Jesus. I had time without little ones to run errands and finish this book.

Benefits of Teaching Classes in Your Home

After a few years of carting my preschoolers with me to teach drawing lessons to groups of homeschoolers, I decided to stay home and teach my own children.

I found teaching in my home has many benefits: I save time, frustration, and money by staying home. I can teach smaller classes and still make the same profit I was making before. It also keeps my house clean when we are all home for the summer—we cannot let it go, because we have two classes three afternoons a week. Having classes Tuesday, Wednesday, and Thursday afternoons gives us long weekends.

Over the last seven years, this has worked well for my family. I bartered with other moms: While I taught their kids in one room, they stayed in back bedrooms to help with my baby and preschoolers if they woke up from their naps during lessons. When I had babies and toddlers, it was refreshing to escape from the mom role and step into the teaching role for a while.

Now I hire my 12-year-old to assist me in class with the young children and my 11-year-old to keep my youngest children in a different part of the house.

Ministry Opportunity of Home Classes

Teaching drawing classes in my home has also been a wonderful opportunity for me to share my faith. I begin each class in prayer, and sometime during each two- to four-week session, I make sure that I pray for each child out loud by name. I have not had a child yet, regardless of background, who has not appreciated blessings being prayed over them. And, surprisingly, I have not had any comments or complaints from parents either.

I usually start off class by asking who has been prayed for, so I can identify whom I will pray for that day. In my class, the closest thing I have ever heard to a squabble has been, "Hey, you're not raising your hand. Mrs. Stull prayed for you. You're trying to get extra prayers!" That kind of squabble is music to my ears.

 WHAT NOW, COACH?

- What skill would you like to teach your children? Can you start a class?
- Do you have a talent for making something that you could sell? If so, could you involve your children in the process?

PREPARATION BRINGS ELATION

When you are a busy mom, the preparation step can be your best friend. In fact, I'd say that preparation brings elation, which is our seventh strategy for turning your family into a dream team. The preparation step can make the difference between disappointment and success, confusion and cooperation, and grumpy kids and happy kids.

APPLICATION

Jump-Start Your Day

I opened my eyes. *Oh no, we overslept!* Hopping out of bed, I rushed to wake the kids. I poured cold milk on cereal, slathered cream cheese on bagels, brushed hair, dispensed vitamins, then tossed sandwiches and fruit into lunch bags.

Dillon and Caleb were riding their bikes to school, but Derek needed me to take him by car, since he was taking his violin and music bag.

It was five minutes before departure time, and I looked down at myself: flannel pajamas and red, furry slippers. And I had no idea what my hair looked like, as I had not glanced in a mirror yet that morning. *Should I get dressed? There's no time. I'll just slip on a coat and go as is. No one will ever know.*

I failed to remember that the day before, while running errands, my car was not quick to start. And my engine had died as I was turning into my driveway that afternoon. *What is going wrong with our nine-year-old SUV?* I wondered to myself. *Of course, car trouble comes when Chris is out of town.*

That morning the car required a few tries before it started, but then we were up and running. Just as we approached the drop-off point, my car died again. *Gas!* I thought. That hadn't even crossed my mind! Heart beating rapidly, I frantically looked at my gas gauge. It registered well below empty!

Again, I glanced down at my crumpled pajamas and furry slippers and then out the window. Mary-Kay-faced moms dressed in cute coordinated outfits held their children's hands as they walked them across the crosswalk.

Then the begging prayers began: "Lord, I know this is all my fault. Please bail me out!" Just then, the car started and I made it home to our gas can on fumes and a prayer. Later that day, I put *more* than 40 gallons of gas into my 40-gallon tank.

Instant Morning Empowerment
- Make your bed.
- Get fully dressed, including makeup.

Dress Affects Attitude and Behavior

It is easy for a stay-at-home mom to think, "I'm just home, so I don't need makeup, and I'll wear my grubbies again today so I don't stain my other clothes." If you have multiple children, this could become your motto for years...if you let it.

However, studies show that the way people dress affects their attitude and behavior. In your wardrobe, include clothes that are practical and comfortable, yet cute too. At home with kids, you will get spilled on or spit up on or worse, so stay away from dry-clean-only clothes (both buying *and* wearing). A few practical, yet nice, coordinating pieces to mix and match go a long way toward sprucing up a wardrobe...and an attitude.

Next, take a look at your face. It only takes a few minutes to stroke on some blush, eyeliner, mascara, and lipstick. Doing so will help you feel more confident and "together." A low-maintenance haircut will help you even more.

Value and Versatility

Does your wardrobe reflect value and versatility? Here are some ideas to keep in mind when shopping and dressing.

- Buy washable clothing to mix and match with other pieces according to the occasion.
- Wear clothing colors that compliment your skin and hair color.
- Keep at least one pair of nice casual shoes for everyday use.
- Dress to impress your husband.

The Rules

We need to say good-bye early to the crumpled pj's and fuzzy slippers and jump-start our days. Make your bed, get dressed for the day in something practical and cute, and put on your makeup. Start your day with confidence, putting your best foot forward.

However, if you have just had a baby, you have your own set of rules. You are not allowed to make the bed until you have taken at least one nap that day. For at least six months, you will be in recovery and survival mode. Once you have survived that period, suit up early each day.

 WHAT NOW, COACH?

- Every morning this week, make up your bed, fix your face, and put on a cute outfit. How does doing so make a difference in your days?
- Identify the wardrobe colors that make you look your best.
- Describe a change you will make in your clothes-buying habits to enhance the versatility of your wardrobe.

The Key Is the Night Before

Just call us Camp Stull. We serve up one plate after another of grub; call out five-minute warnings for dinnertime, bath time, and bedtime; and administer triple antibiotic ointment and adhesive bandages by the boxes. At camp, planning ahead and making a schedule are musts, or total chaos can quickly take over. So it is at our house.

Prepare for the next day by doing everything that can be done the night before. To build your preparation muscles, do the following drills.

Evening Team Drills

1. Perform the kitchen cleanup, helped by KP.
2. Tackle house disorder with a timed five- to ten-minute drill for straightening up.
3. Send campers to the showers (to bathe and brush teeth).
4. Lay out clothes for next day (including socks and shoes).
5. Spray clothes with water bottle mister, and hand press to smooth out wrinkles.
6. Lay out signed permission slips, field trip money, etc.
7. Lay out lunch boxes and dry foods.
8. Check breakfast items for the next morning.
9. Play a mental movie in your head about what things will happen in the morning and throughout the whole day.
10. Place things that must go with you in the driver's seat of the car or in front of the exit door.
11. As needed, post on the refrigerator and bathroom mirror notes with important reminders of things to do in the morning.
12. Share hugs, kisses, and prayers of thankfulness with your loved ones before going to sleep.

Let's chant this together...

> *To peacefully get out the door,*
> *the key is the night before.*

Practicing these drills will lead to bunkhouse blessings and peaceful mornings at your camp too.

 ## WHAT NOW, COACH?

- At least five of seven nights this week, tidy the house and prepare for the next morning before going to bed.
- Write about the evening drills that are the hardest for you to practice and the ones that are the easiest.

What You Need at Your Fingertips

Mary Akers Guyton, in "Mothers: A Field Guide," discusses ways that mothers might be identified by not only appearance but also items they carry with them in order to be prepared. (See chart on next page.) "As a bird watcher looks for an unusual crest or listens carefully for a specific songbird's call," a "mother watcher," she suggests, should be able to spot a woman with young children, even when she does not have her children with her. Guyton goes so far as to identify mothers in specific stages of motherhood by their purse contents.

Guyton says as a mother moves toward maturity, it becomes harder to spot her. She gradually blends back into society.

Spotting a Mother*

Type of Mother	Age of Child	Appearance and Actions	Purse Contents
Hatchling mother	Birth to 6 months	She has dark half-moons under the eyes and a spit-up stain down the back of her left shoulder. Upon hearing someone else's baby cry, she may quickly cross her arms over her chest to stop the involuntary milk let-down reflex.	Baby teething relief gel, liquid acetaminophen with eye-dropper top, and a few birth announcements that have not yet been addressed
Nestling mother	6 to 12 months	She double-ties her shoes, smells faintly of diaper wipes and apple juice, and has one arm much stronger than the other.	A set of brightly colored plastic keys, a slightly smashed package of crackers from the salad bar, and a bent pair of sunglasses
Fledgling mother	12 to 24 months	She will say she needs to go potty or show you her boo-boo. At the end of the day, she falls exhausted into bed and goes night-night.	A crayon fragment and part of the grocery store's free cookie sample wrapped in a napkin
Juvenile mother	2 to 5 years	She wears a cartoon-character bandage on her finger and has a ketchup-colored hand print streaked across her sleeve. When driving, she sings with gusto, "The Wheels on the Bus."	Triple antibiotic ointment, a straw, and a Barbie shoe and/or Hot Wheels car

*Adapted from Mary Akers Guyton, "Mothers: A Field Guide," *Home Educator's Family Times* 9, no. 2 (2001); available at http://www.homeeducator.com/FamilyTimes/articles/9-2article14.htm.

What a Mother Needs

Mothers need to be prepared for a number of situations in a myriad of venues. One way to be prepared at home is to keep pertinent information handy in one notebook.

Contents for a Know-It Notebook

- Team and class rosters
- Daily class schedules
- Teachers' phone numbers
- Neighborhood phone numbers
- School information sheets
- Church office numbers
- Fitness center class schedule
- List of babysitters with their phone numbers
- List for babysitter to use: emergency numbers, allergies listed, bedtimes listed, likes/dislikes of children
- Pockets for pending things: birthday party invitations (address and/or directions), Bible verse memorization sheets, and fund-raiser papers and flyers

Being Prepared Away from Home

- **Keep frequently called numbers in your cell phone.** Though you may not call your neighbors frequently, having their home and cell phone numbers in your cell phone in case of emergency is a good idea.
- **Keep a first-aid kit in the car at all times.** Kits can be purchased in the pharmacy section of discount retailers. Kits include bandages, triple antibiotic ointment, sting/bite wipes, gauze, and tape.
- **Keep handy wipes in the car.** Use them to clean hands after being in public places. They are also convenient to have for those away-from-home diaper changes.
- **Keep in the car backpacks filled with small toys, crayons, and paper.** At older siblings' sporting events, lay out a blanket for little ones to play on with their toys. A few snacks and drinks will help even more.

When the mother watchers get out their binoculars, will they be able to identify you correctly? Most likely they'll identify you as organized and blessed.

 ## WHAT NOW, COACH?

- Record your plan for creating a know-it notebook. List some things you will keep in the notebook. Then do it.
- Add important numbers to your cell phone contact list.
- Be sure your car is stocked with needs: first-aid kit, wipes, and a backpack full of activities.

APPLICATION
46

What's for Dinner?

Oh no, it's 4:00 P.M. and I have seven mouths to feed for dinner! What will we have? Trying to stir up positive thoughts, I grab the recipe book and thumb through the pages. *Easy but Elegant Chicken—this looks great!* I slide my finger down the list of ingredients. *Oops, don't have green onions.* Still hopeful, I turn the page. *Pasta Con Broccoli...yum! But I am missing heavy cream.* A few pages back, a quiche recipe catches my eye. But not only am I still missing green onions—I have no mushrooms or half-and-half, and the bacon is still in the freezer.

About that time, in comes a son. "What's for dinner?" he innocently asks.

"What's it to you?" the defensive, guilt-ridden, and frustrated mother (that's me) answers.

Menu Planning

Can you relate? If so, you are not alone. I recently heard that 60 percent of moms do not know at 4:00 P.M. what they are serving their family for dinner that night.

Getting past the dinner preparation blues is easy when ingredients are on hand. All it takes is planning ahead.

One type of menu planner lists breakfast, lunch, and dinner across the top of the paper and the days of the week down the left side. There is nothing difficult about it—the hardest part is keeping the *one doing the planning* (yourself) disciplined to use the tool over the long run.

Deciding *what* to fix is as hard as anything. We want the meals to be nutritious, yet foods the kids will eat. I heard one mom say that she hopes ketchup is a vegetable, because it is the only one her child will eat.

Keep in mind the week's schedule as you assign dinners to the evenings. For open nights, plan to make the entrées that are more time intensive. For nights filled with activities, plan quick, easy meals.

After planning the meals for the week, look at the recipes, check your current pantry and refrigerator stock, and note what ingredients you need to buy. If you are on a two-week plan, prepare meals using fresh produce early in the first week. If needed, make another quick grocery shopping stop for fresh foods only.

If you want help in your menu planning, search the Internet for "menu planning" or "family dinner planning." A number of sites will be listed. At some sites, you can sign up for weekly menus for about a dollar a week; shopping lists are usually included. Some of these lists can be reformatted to fit your own needs. Here are a few interesting sites that offer email helps for a dollar or less a week:

- **The Six O'Clock Scramble:** This site offers a Wednesday email newsletter with five quick entrée recipes with fresh side dish suggestions. Included is a shopping list that can be reformatted to drop unwanted recipes. (Available at *thescramble.com*.)
- **Dine Without Whine:** Each Thursday, members receive by email recipes for seven entrées and a few desserts, side dishes, and kid-friendly snacks and brunches. A shopping list and a humorous blog are also provided. (Available at *dinewithoutwhine.com*.)

- **Saving Dinner:** This site offers menu mailers with five or six entrées and side dish recipes that fit your family's preferences (low fat, vegetarian, etc.). (Available at *savingdinner.com*.)

To Eat or Not to Eat

Even when you are mindful of the varied likes and dislikes of the multiple family members as you plan the meals, it is not unusual for someone to not want to eat the prepared meal. What are the options in that case? Options for children who do not want to eat the prepared meal might include these:

- If over age three, they may get for themselves raw fruits and vegetables as a substitute.
- They may eat leftovers from the night before.
- They could even eat nothing, but no snacks or dessert would be allowed.

Experts agree that forcing children to clean their plate often has negative effects when trying to train the children to have good eating habits, and this practice can lead to obesity later in life. So pick your battles wisely.

Modeling healthy eating habits is important. Keep bowls of fruit and other healthy foods visible, and if you choose to buy sweets, keep them hidden away from little eyes until you choose to serve them.

Dinner Winners

Simple dinners are winners. Most children prefer food in its purest form (not "casseroled" up) and *not touching* other food on the plate. Simple dinners consisting of a meat, baby carrots, rolls, green beans, and a fruit are often well accepted and the healthiest—the best all around. Paper plates can simplify dinner even more; use them on busy days or days when you have already used enough dishes to fill a dishwasher.

Recently, I reveled in the joy of a successful simple dinner. Chris was out of town, and it was a cold day. I had spent most of the afternoon writing and needed to make something quick and easy. I set the table with a white plastic tablecloth and lit some candles as our centerpiece. We ate hot old-fashioned oatmeal, grapes, and toasted bagels on china and drank white grape juice from goblets. What started out as an unplanned meal ended up being a delightful meal that everyone enjoyed.

Here are some other quickies:

- Rotisserie chicken from the grocery store served with raw vegetables and bread
- Frozen pizza and salad

Every family has several favorite dinners—dinner winners. Homemade chicken noodle soup is one of ours.

BRENNA'S EASY HOMEMADE CHICKEN NOODLE SOUP

8 cups water
8 chicken bouillon cubes
3 large carrots, diced
3 celery stalks, diced
1 onion, diced
1 tablespoon minced garlic (optional)
3 cooked chicken breasts, diced or shredded
    (boil breasts or substitute one precooked chicken)
3 cups wide egg noodles
Salt and pepper

In a large pan, bring water to a boil. Add bouillon cubes, diced vegetables, and garlic. Boil for 15 minutes or until vegetables are tender. Add noodles and boil for the amount of time specified on the package. Lower heat and add chicken. Add water if needed to make it more soupy. Add salt and pepper to taste. Makes 8 servings. Easy, yummy, and great for your health.

Here are a few more of my family's favorites:

- Breakfast for dinner (scrambled eggs, sausage, biscuits, fruit, and yogurt)
- Grilled chicken, steak, or pork chops served with mashed potatoes, green beans, salad, and bread
- Tacos, salad, tortilla chips, and salsa

Creative Touches

As you plan the meals, be creative. When trying to make a dinner special, give attention to presentation. Children will eat almost any food cut or formed into a fun shape and displayed on a brightly colored plate. During the Easter season, add some green sprinkles and a few jelly beans on top of a bowl of oatmeal. Fill a waffle cone with diced fresh fruit for a fun and healthy summer dessert. Use food coloring for holidays to make green leprechaun milk and pink valentine milk.

Spice up your family meals in a whole new way. When your children say, "Mom, what's for dinner?" you will answer them with a confident smile.

 WHAT NOW, COACH?

- List your family's favorite fast and nutritious meals you can prepare at home.
- Record your dinner menu plans for the next week. Vary some from your usuals.
- When your menu is planned, inventory your pantry and refrigerator, and then make a grocery list.

APPLICATION
47

Grocery Shopping in a Snap

Two young boys walked into a grocery store, picked up a box of tampons, and proceeded to the checkout counter.

The man at the counter asked the older boy, "Son, how old are you?"

"Eight," the boy replied.

The man continued, "Do you know how these are used?"

The boy replied, "Not exactly, but they aren't for me. They are for my brother. He's four. We saw on TV that if you use these you would be able to swim and ride a bike. He can't do either one."

Not Usually Funny or Fun

That story, which I received over email, made me chuckle about grocery shopping. But I do not usually chuckle about shopping.

Grocery stores are looking for ways to help. Some stores offer free child care while mom shops. By doing so, they free up cart space dramatically for their customers. Studies show that factor alone will make people spend more. How many times have you walked in with a baby in the carrier and fastened the carrier to the cart, put your two-year-old and the diaper bag in the back of the cart, only to think, *Now where will I put the groceries?*

Does the trip always seem to take a little longer than you anticipate? By the end, the newborn is screaming for the next feeding, and the potty-training two-year-old is simultaneously saying, "I have to go…*now!*"

Tips for Grocery Shopping

Go alone. Whenever possible, try to go to the store without small children or with as few as possible.

Take a list. The good news is that if you are applying what we discussed in the last section about meal planning, you have a plan and your shopping list is made out.

When you use a shopping list, not only will you spend less on impulse purchases, you will also have fewer repurchases of food already stocked in your pantry and freezer. If you are working on a two-week plan, you will make fewer trips and spend less.

Design a sample grocery list on your computer and print as needed. If you organize the list to show items in the order they are stocked on the grocery store shelves, you can easily see what you need when you get to the produce department, cereal aisle, frozen foods, pharmacy, pet products, etc.

Save money by warehouse shopping. This is especially helpful if you have a large family or need large amounts of certain foods. Warehouse stores have great buys also on gifts around holidays, and their name-brand clothes cost a fraction of what they cost in retail stores.

Save money by ad matching. Some discount stores will match competitors' front-page sale prices. At checkout, present the competitors' current ads along with the items, and the checker will ring up those items for the advertised prices.

Stock up on foods when they are on sale. For example, turkeys are inexpensive during the Thanksgiving and Christmas seasons; buy extras and keep them frozen until needed.

Save money with coupons. If you are a coupon cutter, you will find that coupon savings can really add up over time. Buy multiple Sunday papers, collate the coupon sections, then cut out multiple coupons all at once. Having multiple coupons will increase your savings in the store on items you frequently use. Don't forget to look for coupons on the Internet; print coupons from Web sites such as *boodle.com, smartsource.com,* and *coolsavings.com.* Also check manufacturers' Web sites for products you frequently use.

Review
- Make out a menu.
- Inventory the pantry and refrigerator.

- Go grocery shopping with a list.
- Refuse to pay full price: Shop at warehouses, ad match, or use coupons.

Groceries—everyone's gotta have them. If possible, go grocery shopping alone, or go with the fewest number of children possible. If you are not in survival mode, you might consider gleaning the fruit from the money tree located inside Sunday newspapers: *coupons.*

 ## WHAT NOW, COACH?

- Once your grocery list is ready, consider where you can get the best values.
- Clip or print out coupons for items on your list or things you buy regularly.
- Then go shopping. Did I mention to go without children?

Free Home Shopping Network

Want to shop at home for free? Anticipate your gift needs, and buy items on sale at a time convenient for you. That will allow you to conveniently shop at home "for free" when a gift need arises.

Prepurchase Gifts and Cards
Having gifts, cards, and wrapping supplies on hand leads to calmly and confidently celebrating special events. You will save time *and* money. Preparation brings elation.

- **Gift box, pantry, or closet:** Keep gifts on hand that can be ready for the giving when a special occasion comes:

Baby gifts

Wedding gifts

Children's birthday gifts (age appropriate
to your child/children)

Friend gifts

Seasonal gifts

- **Prize basket or bin:** Keep prizes on hand so children can "shop" to spend money earned by doing chores (detailed in chapter 1).

- **Greeting card file:** Having cards on hand will encourage diligence in acknowledging others' special life moments. Buying or making cards ahead of the time needed saves time and money. You will want to have some on hand for all occasions:

    Birthday (for adult and child)

    Anniversary

    Thank you

    Get well

    Sympathy

    Baby

    Friendship

    Blank

Make Personalized Cards

Use a photo of your child to design special cards for family and friends. One year I took a picture of two-year-old Dillon in a bright red wagon; he was holding a big heart-shaped sign that said *Happy Valentine's Day*. I used that photo to create cards.

If you are at the beach, write *THANKS* in the sand and have each child sit or lie behind it to have a photograph made. Put the pictures on halved and folded 8½-by-11-inch card stock, and let the children use these cards to write thank-you notes for presents or to teachers throughout the year. Are you too far from the beach? Here's an alternative: Instead of writing *THANKS* in the sand, write it on the sidewalk with sidewalk chalk.

Cherish those persons God has placed in your life. Remember them on their special days and for their special contributions to your life.

> *Preparation brings elation*
> *when you are ready for celebrations.*

 WHAT NOW, COACH?

- Designate a box, bin, or closet for storing a variety of prepurchased gifts.
- Watch for sale items, and begin to collect gifts.

APPLICATION

Prepare to Feed Your Soul

How would you describe your relationship with God? Do you know Jesus Christ personally, or are you still in the process of discovering who He is? Do you desire to have a sense of walking with God each day, knowing that He has prepared a way for you?

"If you are weary of some sleepy form of devotion, probably God is as weary of it as you are," said Frank Laubach (*Practicing His Presence*). "Shake out of it, and approach Him in one of the countless fresh directions."

Purpose to keep your mind fixed on Christ. Do this by living a life of love for His sake as you change diapers, wipe the kitchen counter for the nineteenth time in a day, and clip ten fingernails and ten toenails for each child after bath time. God is present with you all the time. Carry on conversations with Him throughout the day. Establishing that habit takes effort; you must *will* your thoughts in that direction.

Another holy habit is setting aside time to pray and read the Bible. Have a structure and a plan for prayertime and time in God's Word. Oswald Chambers said, "Prayer does not fit us for the greater works; prayer *is* the greater work" (*My Utmost for His Highest,* October 17). It takes discipline.

One of the motivating thoughts I tell myself is this: *"The Almighty God, Creator of the universe, wants to meet with me. Will I pass up the opportunity today?"*

A Prayer Notebook

When I was in my mid-20s, this disheartening realization hit me: My prayer life, which I consider to be of great importance, was sporadic and unorganized. I prayed and asked the Lord for some direction on what I should do.

Shortly after that, I read a magazine article by inspirational speaker and author Becky Tirabassi. She shared how journaling her prayers to God had provided structure and a plan for her prayer life and time in God's Word. I then knew that I needed to make my own prayer notebook.

I bought a small notebook, filled it with blank notebook paper, and divided it into sections: "Praise," "Thanksgiving," "Confession," "Lifting Up (Requests)," and "God's Words to Me" (Bible verses that speak to my heart). This notebook is now a tool that aids my spiritual growth. This tool helps to keep me focused as I pray, since I am I writing my thoughts to God. And it helps me take heed to God's words to me, as I write down the things that stand out to me.

As I come across Scriptures pertaining to the sections in the notebook, I write them in at the beginning of the section. I often incorporate the verses into my daily prayers.

Here are some examples of Scriptures I have written in my notebook:

Confession Section

Search me, O God, and know my heart;
test me and know my anxious thoughts.
See if there is any offensive way in me,
and lead me in the way everlasting.
—Psalm 139:23–24

Who can discern his errors?
Forgive my hidden faults.
Keep your servant also from willful sins;
may they not rule over me.
Then will I be blameless,
innocent of great transgression.
May the words of my mouth and the meditation of my heart
be pleasing in your sight,
O LORD, my Rock and my Redeemer.
—Psalm 19:12–14

Lifting Up (Requests) Section

In the morning, O LORD, you hear my voice;
in the morning I lay my requests before you
and wait in expectation.
—Psalm 5:3

Now to him who is able to do immeasurably more than all we
ask or imagine, according to his power that is at work within us,
to him be glory in the church and in Christ Jesus throughout all
generations, for ever and ever! Amen.
—Ephesians 3:20–21

God's Word to Me Section
I am especially fond of *The Living Bible*'s paraphrase of
Psalm 119. I use parts of it as a prayer before doing my
Bible reading for the day.

Open my eyes to see wonderful things in your Word. I am but
a pilgrim here on earth: how I need a map—and your commands
are my chart and guide. I long for your instructions more than
I can tell....

Just tell me what to do and I will do it, Lord. As long as I live
I'll wholeheartedly obey.

—Psalm 119:18–20, 33–34 (TLB)

Personalize a prayer notebook or use whatever will turn your focus and attention to experiencing God and who He is. A notebook or any other method in and of itself is useless unless the use of it draws you into deeper relationship with God. Hand in hand with the Bible, tools can help you connect with God. Regularly feeding your mind with the truths of Christ will bring joy to your heart and soul and purpose to your life.

Missed "Meals," Missed Fellowship

Once you have a tool in place for spiritual growth, preparation can bring elation. But you must also remind yourself not to allow preparation to bring condemnation when you don't meet your goals in using that tool.

When I had a one-year-old, a three-year-old, and two early-elementary, energetic boys, getting myself back into a routine of a daily time of prayer and Bible reading was difficult. I was discouraged with my inconsistent quiet times. Most of my prayers focused on praying that the baby would sleep through the night and that God would help me.

I tried not to feel guilty, knowing that God would not want that. But I knew I was missing out on precious fellowship with my heavenly Father.

I had finally decided my daily prayertime was not going to happen unless I rose earlier in the morning. I am *not* a morning person, but I knew I needed to nurture my relationship with the Lord and needed His strength to serve my family.

One morning, I woke up at 5:30 A.M. (a miracle in itself), wrapped my snuggly robe around me, and shuffled in my slippers to the living room. I expectantly knelt in prayer beside the couch, and just as I breathed a "Good morning, Lord," I heard little footsteps toddling down the hall from the bedrooms. My heart sank.

Maybe if I ignore him, he'll go away, I thought, then said to the Lord, "Lord, even when I get up at 5:30 in the morning, I can't seem to get any time alone with You!" Just then, the Lord spoke to my heart, *"Whoever welcomes the little children welcomes me."* (See Mark 9:37.)

I turned around, tears streaming down my face, hugged my child tightly, and knew that I was communing with God.

It is great to have a plan and to be prepared to grow closer to God. But, no matter how great the plan and determination, we moms do not know what a day will bring. Actually, that's one great reason to have your prayertime first thing in the morning, the time least likely to be interrupted or thrown off track. But even that can be thwarted.

In *Practicing His Presence*, Frank Laubach said, "And if you should forget Him for minutes or even days, do not groan or repent, but begin anew with a smile. Every minute can be a fresh beginning."

I tell myself, "I missed out yesterday (and a number of other days) on what God may have wanted to tell me through His Word. But today is a new day, and He is waiting and wanting to meet with me. What will my decision be *today*?"

God understands where you are. He knows everything that you are up against—every emotional struggle, every physical struggle, every worry and care you have, and all the people you are responsible for. A verse that was especially encouraging to me during the physically demanding days of having a newborn was Isaiah 40:11: *"He tends his flock like a shepherd: He gathers the lambs in his arms and carries them close to his heart; **he gently leads those that have young"** (bold added for emphasis).

God knows how hard it is—sleep deprivation, colicky babies, continuous feeding and changing of the baby, work that never ends, whiney children, money that runs out before the month does—and the Great Shepherd is gently whispering to you of His love and care, provision, and direction. Trust Him with all that you are—follow Him.

 ## WHAT NOW, COACH?

- Design a personal tool for spiritual growth. Use it hand in hand with the Bible.
- Identify several Scriptures that speak to your heart in your current state of motherhood. Keep them ever before your eyes, in your mouth, and in your heart.

A PEACE-FILLED HEART AND HOME

In the last seven sections, we've discussed strategies for organizing your family in such a way that everyone wins: the parents, the kids, the home, and all those in your path.

We may fool ourselves into thinking that with winning strategies, good intentions, optimism, hard work, and discipline, we can control our lives. But no matter how much we try on our own, this life will never work well enough to create the inner peace we all seek. True peace comes with faith in God.

None of the spiritual disciplines we've talked about are in and of themselves ways to making peace with God—not hours of reciting prayers every day, not reading and memorizing the Bible, not doing good works, not going to church.

The problem goes back to the beginnings of the earth. God made the world and everything in it. He created the first man and woman, Adam and Eve, and placed them in an earthly paradise, the garden in Eden. But because of the man and woman's disobedience, sin entered the world, and humans have struggled with it ever since. But God made a way for us to have peace with Him once again through the death and resurrection of His Son, Jesus Christ.

The Story of My Road to Peace

I was a little girl when I realized my dire need for a Savior. I may have been very young, but my sins were quickly stacking up. I was already a strong-willed, selfish little manipulator.

I'm second born in a set of triplets. Early on, I earned the name Captain, according to my mom and dad (I didn't find out about that until I was in my 20s). My parents tell stories of me as a two-year-old sitting in a chair for hours because they told me I would have to apologize for something I'd done if I wanted to get out of the chair.

As a seven-year-old, my heart began to open up to things of God. I learned that the Bible says, *"All have sinned and fall short of the glory of God"* (Romans 3:23) and that Jesus is the only way to God (John 4:16). John 3:16 spoke to my heart: *"For God so loved the world that he gave his one and only Son, that whoever believes in him shall not perish but have eternal life."* My dad shared with me that salvation is a gift from God and cannot be earned on good merits (Ephesians 2:8–9).

When I received God's gift of salvation and gave all that I was to the Lord, He changed me into a new person. He started directing that strong will into good things. In Jesus Christ, who *is* the Way, the Truth, and the Life (John 14:6), I found true inner joy and discovered the meaning of life.

In the last 30 years, He has been my peace, purpose, and joy throughout all the ups and downs. His unconditional love and care have been my strength and hope—even through all my mistakes and acts of stupidity.

Keep God at the Center

God wants you to place Him at the center of your heart, soul, and desires. That can be especially challenging for a mom, who has the responsibility for the constant daily care of the family, such as what they will eat, wear, and do. Jesus said for us not to worry about that stuff: *"Seek first the kingdom of God and His righteousness, and all these things shall be added to you"* (Matthew 6:33 NKJV). When we seek first the kingdom of God, our needs—food, clothing, and such—will be met; we have no need to worry.

As you hurry through your days, God consistently and gently pursues you out of His great love. God knows and cares for every detail about you and your life. Maybe you are paralyzed between the monotony of tasks in the home and busyness of outside activities. Or you may be guilt ridden about the anger that spews from your mouth toward your children when you least expect it. Or you may feel frustrated and discouraged because it seems you live in a chaotic whirlwind every day. God hurts with you in the painful and discouraging times and wants to offer you His comfort, love, and hope—His peace.

When I started writing this book, my children were ten months, two years, four years, seven years, and nine years old. I know, understand, and live with the daily chaos of small children in the home. My home is spinning with activity most of the time, but I can say we have an underlying peace in our home and a deep peace in our hearts that springs from a true inner joy.

Home Life: Mundane to Meaningful

The Bible says, *"Whatever you do, work at it with all your heart, as working for the Lord, not for men"* (Colossians 3:23). As a mom, that is motivating to me when I realize that everything I do for my family, I do for the Lord.

If my motive is love for God, no amount of ingratitude from my family can hinder my service in the home. When I have my rubber-glove-clad hands in sudsy water tackling dirty pots and pans and manage to keep a joyful attitude, the Lord is interested and pleased. When I'm lying on my tummy patiently working with a child on the alphabet puzzle and reciting phonic sounds for the tenth time in one day, the Lord is interested and pleased. When I'm stirring, with love, a big steamy pot of homemade chicken noodle soup, the Lord is interested and pleased.

Oswald Chambers said, the goal is "to be exceptional in the ordinary things" (*My Utmost for His Highest*, October 21). You can do this every day in the midst of real living—as you patiently wipe up spilled milk, put a work project on hold to stay home with an ill child, manage to maintain a positive attitude as you fold *another* load of laundry, thoughtfully speak an encouraging word to a neighbor, or keep your cool when your two-year-old is throwing a temper tantrum on the floor and you are queasy with morning sickness.

Does being *exceptional* mean being a perfect mom? No. No one can be a perfect mom. But we've looked at hundreds of ways to be a good mom.

My young friend Marcia shared this prayer with me shortly after losing her husband to cancer. It reflects my heart and the heart of this book:

For the Day

Almighty God,
We bless and praise Thee that we have awakened
to the light of another earthly day;
and now we will think of what a day should be.
Our days are Thine, let them be spent for Thee.
Our days are few, let them be spent with care.
There are dark days behind us, forgive their sinfulness;
there may be dark days before us, strengthen us for
their trials.
We pray Thee to shine on this day—the day which
we may call our own.

Lord,
We go to our daily work;
help us to take pleasure therein.
Show us clearly what our duty is;
help us to be faithful in doing it.
Let all we do be done well, fit for Thine eye to see.
Give us strength to do, patience to bear;
let our courage never fail.

When we cannot love our work, let us think of it as
Thy task;
and, by our true love to Thee,
make unlovely things shine in the light of Thy great love.
Amen.
—George Dawson (1821–1876)

Are you stuck in a rut of regretting the past and fretting about the future? Don't fear that your life will end—fear that it will never begin.

So tickle your children until they can stand it no more, laugh until your stomach muscles ache, give hugs freely, cheer loudly when your child is up to bat, sing in the shower, and pray like you've never prayed before. Say "I love you" often and "I forgive you" and "I was wrong" as needed. Hold your husband in your arms and tell him he's the best.

Embrace today with joy—this is what God gave you.

Dear Reader:

I have been praying for you as you read this book—praying that God will work in your heart and home.

I am interested in knowing what is going on in your life. To contact me or to learn more about my ministry, go to www.Brennastull.com.

Brenna Stull
Coach Mom

BIBLIOGRAPHY

Aslett, Don. *How to Handle 1,000 Things at Once: A Fun Guide to Mastering Home and Personal Management.* New York: MJF Books, 1997.

Barnes, Emilie. *The 15-Minute Organizer.* Eugene, OR: Harvest House Publishers, 2003.

Bounds, Edward M. *Power Through Prayer.* Grand Rapids, MI: Zondervan Publishing House, 26th printing of revised edition 1962–1982.

Briscoe, Jill. *Daily Study Bible for Women: New Living Translation.* Wheaton, IL: Tyndale House Publishers, 1999.

Briscoe, Jill. *Prayer That Works.* Wheaton, IL: Tyndale House Publishers, 2000.

Brother Lawrence and Frank Charles Laubach. *Practicing His Presence.* Beaumont, TX: The SeedSowers, 1973.

Brown, Margaret Wise; illustrated by Clement Hurd. *Goodnight Moon.* New York: HarperFestival, 1991.

Carle, Eric. *The Very Hungry Caterpillar.* New York: Philomel Books, 1994, 1969.

Chambers, Oswald. *My Utmost for His Highest.* Westwood, NJ: Barbour and Co, 1963.

Christenson, Evelyn. *What Happens When Women Pray.* Colorado Springs: Life Journey, 2004.

Hislop, Beverly White. *Shepherding a Woman's Heart: A New Model for Effective Ministry to Women.* Chicago: Moody Publishers, 2003.

Hughes, Selwyn, and Larry Dyke. *Light for the Path*. Every Day Light Series. Nashville: Broadman and Holman Publishers, 1999.

Karp, Harvey. *The Happiest Toddler on the Block: The New Way to Stop the Daily Battle of Wills and Raise a Secure and Well-Behaved One- to Four-Year-Old*. New York: Bantam Books, 2004.

Kelleher, Nancy. "Literacy Begins at Home: Research Shows Conversation and Shared Reading Make the Difference: Family Dinner's the Winner." *Boston Herald*, December 10, 1996.

Kimmel, Tim. *Raising Kids Who Turn Out Right*. Sisters, OR: Multnomah Press, 1993, 1989.

Kurcinka, Mary Sheedy. *Sleepless in America: Is Your Child Misbehaving or Missing Sleep?* New York: HarperCollins, 2006.

Loehr, James E., and Tony Schwartz. *The Power of Full Engagement: Managing Energy, Not Time, Is the Key to High Performance and Personal Renewal*. New York: Free Press, 2003.

Lotz, Anne Graham. *AnGeL Ministries Newsletter,* Spring 2005.

Lucado, Max. *God Thinks You're Wonderful*. Nashville: J. Countryman, 2003.

McLaughlin, Andrew T. "Family Dinners Provide Food for Thought As Well." *Boston Herald*, March 14, 1996.

Ortberg, John, and Ruth Haley Barton. *An Ordinary Day with Jesus: Experiencing the Reality of God in Your Everyday Life*. Grand Rapids, MI: Zondervan, 2001

Otto, Donna. *Get More Done in Less Time*. Eugene, OR: Harvest House Publishers, 1995.

Piper, John. *A Hunger for God*. Wheaton, IL: Crossway Books, 1997.

Peterson, Eugene H. *The Message: The New Testament in Contemporary English*. Colorado Springs: NavPress, 1993.

Rosemond, John K. *John Rosemond's Six-Point Plan for Raising Happy, Healthy Children*. Kansas City, KS: Andrews and McMeel, Universal Press Syndicate Co., 1989.

Rosenfeld, Alvin, and Nicole Wise. *The Over-Scheduled Child*. New York: St. Martin's Press, 2000.

Warren, Richard. *The Purpose-Driven Life: What on Earth Am I Here For?* Grand Rapids, MI: Zondervan, 2002.

Young, Ed. *Kid CEO: How to Keep Your Children from Running Your Life.* New York: Warner Books, 2004.

New Hope® Publishers is a division of WMU®,
an international organization that challenges Christian believers
to understand and be radically involved in God's mission.
For more information about WMU, go to www.wmu.com.
More information about New Hope books may be found
at www.newhopepublishers.com. New Hope books
may be purchased at your local bookstore.

Other Books for MOMS

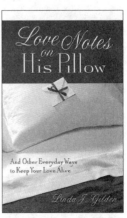
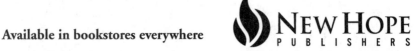